The Selling of Mary Davies
and Other Writings

The Selling of
Mary Davies
and Other Writings

SIMON
JENKINS

JOHN MURRAY

© Simon Jenkins 1993

First published in 1993
by John Murray (Publishers) Ltd.,
50 Albemarle Street, London W1X 4BD

The moral right of the author has been asserted

A catalogue record for this book is available
from the British Library

ISBN 0-7195-4860-8

Typeset in Linotron 11½/13½pt Times
by Rowland Phototypesetting Ltd.,
Bury St Edmunds, Suffolk
Printed and bound in Great Britain at
the University Press, Cambridge

For my father

CONTENTS

ILLUSTRATIONS

PREFACE

THIS BOOK is mostly about London. It is about the people who built London and those who have rebuilt it, landowners, architects, conservers and destroyers. More than any other great city, London has always argued with its past. These writings are meant to shed light on that argument. They also reflect my interest in art, architecture and writing beyond London's boundaries, in Britain generally and in Europe. The book begins with the tale of 'The Selling of Mary Davies'. Hers was the sort of accident on which so much of London's history has turned. As a baby she inherited the Manor of Ebury in Westminster just when the city began to grow after the Great Fire of 1666. She swiftly became one of Britain's most desirable matrimonial properties. The family that bought her, the Grosvenors of Cheshire, founded an estate in London that was to last three centuries. An Act of Parliament giving its tenants the right of freehold is bringing that era to an end.

The builders and developers on whom such estates relied were always controversial. From Nash and Cubitt under the Regency to the property booms and slumps of recent years, London's growth was based not so much on wealth as on bankruptcy. Its streets have never been paved with gold, they have been paved with insolvency notices. From Chester Square to Kensington Palace Gardens, from Ladbroke Grove to the cliff faces of the Isle of Dogs, London is the creation of 'The Great Bankrupts'. They are with us still.

I have watched London's arguments in good company. Two dominant influences were Nikolaus Pevsner and John Betjeman, to each of whom I devote a chapter. The first is recalled in an

ix

appreciation, the second in his own favourite genre, the architectural walk. If any spirit infuses these writings, it is that of Betjeman. I still find myself seeing the city through his eyes, sometimes loving, sometimes wickedly sceptical. We went on countless architectural tours. 'Betjeman's Heathrow' is an account of one of them. Betjeman had a term of art for any large modern building that he found ugly; he called it a 'Seifert'. The cause of his scorn, the architect Richard Seifert, is now in his eighties. His impact on the postwar metropolis has been second to none. Some have compared it with that of Sir Christopher Wren. Wherever we turn there is a 'Seifert' standing and another on the rise. But has Seifert built anything that we might one day want to preserve? 'Seifert's Towers' offers an answer.

Some architects aspire to the state of artists. Others are seen as monsters. In both incarnations they are by far the most important figures in London's development. They determine more than its appearance. Their skill, enthusiasm and prejudice decide how people use a city, whether they will love or hate it. From the past I discuss Cubitt's Belgravia and Wyatville's Windsor Castle, from the present Robert Venturi's National Gallery, Quinlan Terry's Richmond and the protagonists in the Battle of the Styles. This battle, which raged throughout the 1980s, polarized on the opposing personalities of the Prince of Wales and the leaders of 'neo-Modernism'. It reached a crisis in the Prince's Hampton Court speech of 1984. 'The Prince and the Architect', '*Veni, Vidi*, Venturi' and 'The Great Fire of Windsor' examine aspects of that remarkable royal intervention.

A wider gulf divides the London built by these architects from that sought and seen by the visitor. To the tourist, historic cities are not places in which to live and work, but places for leisure and entertainment. Tourists are increasingly seen not as an economic opportunity but as an environmental menace. The cliché of the Eighties was that Britain, indeed the whole of Europe, was becoming one continuous 'theme park'. Certainly tourism is growing and must one day outstrip the capacity of many popular sites. The historian David Lowenthal has described the past as 'a foreign country, with the thriving tourist industry'. We seek ever more relics of the past, and would object were we to find them rationed or closed to us. Yet we also object to the millions who wish to join in our search. In 'Thank God for Tourists' I consider what mass tourism may mean for the museums and galleries bequeathed us by the Victorians. In 'The Cult of the Ruin' and 'Death on the Nile' I look at two cases where science and politics are undermining the role of the traditional museum: the restored temples of the Acropolis and the dispersed antiquities of Egypt.

Like Mr Pickwick I find respite from controversy in the by-ways of the past, in John Constable and the print-makers of Hampstead, in the old churchyards of the City and in the curious story of the Vale of Health. I am diverted by happenings: the theft and return of the Kenwood Vermeer; the visit of Goya's *Countess of Chinchón* to the National Gallery; the removal of the Leonardo copy from the Royal Academy to Magdalen College; James Lees-Milne's early acquisitions for the National Trust. I have also included some pieces that are tangential to my theme, on the fate of geography and grammar in schools. These are all fragments of history that should not pass unsung. With the demise of metropolitan government, London has lost its democratic forum. It cannot debate with itself. The capital is too big for the village Hampdens of the boroughs, yet too parochial for the gods of Westminster and the media. (The old *Evening Standard* at least keeps a tattered flag on the London mast.) The metropolis has no definitive voice.

A few of these essays have appeared before and been expanded or rewritten. 'Betjeman's Heathrow' began as a piece in the *Evening Standard* in 1973. 'The Cult of the Ruin' followed a visit to Athens in 1987 for *The Sunday Times*. Versions also appeared in that paper of 'The Countess of Chinchón' and 'Dr Syntax'. 'Cinderella Geography' started life as a talk to the Geographical Association in 1992. 'The Great Bankrupts' was LWT's London Lecture the same year. 'In a City Churchyard' formed the introduction to Harvey Hackman's 1981 book on that subject, published by Collins. 'Thank God for Tourists' expands an article that appeared in the *TLS* in 1989. The pieces on Vermeer, Leonardo, Egypt and the National Trust are based on articles for *The Times*. To all their publishers I express my thanks.

1

THE SELLING OF
MARY DAVIES

THE HOUSE of Lords was the right place for the drama. The 41-year-old Duke of Westminster stood arms akimbo on the steps of the throne. His face ill-concealed his anger. He was appalled as his peers, barely his peers, allowed themselves to be whipped through the lobbies by the government of the day. The richest man in England found it beneath his dignity to speak. The innocently titled Housing and Urban Development Bill was unstoppable. It was to strip him and at least four of his noble colleagues of sovereignty over their London estates by allowing their tenants to convert leases into freeholds without let or hindrance. As the bill wended its way into law, he made the only gesture he felt open to him. He cancelled his Conservative party membership.

Inherited wealth, like inherited beauty, encourages all the deadly sins in those who possess it – and in those who wish they did. Yet even inheritance has its price. It can be acquired with money. It can be bartered. It can be stolen for love or it can be married. In the late seventeenth century, the states of Europe were pieced together, and sometimes torn asunder, by dynastic marriages. London was being formed the same way. For half a century civil war, Restoration, plague, fire and Glorious Revolution upheaved Stuart society. A new nobility was formed and

1

this nobility sought wealth appropriate to its status. Nowhere was wealth so tantalizingly to hand as in the fields west and north of the Cities of London and Westminster. These fields stood ready to house a metropolis that no longer needed to defend itself against invasion and was less susceptible to the terrors that had recently devastated the old City.

The quickest way of acquiring wealth is by theft. The next quickest is by marriage. The accidents of birth and death had brought the fields of West London into the possession of a succession of heiresses who soon became the most sought-after brides in the land. In 1669 Rachel, daughter of the 4th Earl of Southampton, inherited the ancient manor of Bloomsbury, granted her family by Henry VIII. A marriage was arranged to William Wriothesley, son and heir to the 5th Earl and 1st Duke of Bedford, whose home at Woburn was supplemented by land on the Strand at Covent Garden. The descendants of this union, the Bedford family, hold the Bloomsbury estate to this day.

In 1711 another young lady, Henrietta Cavendish Holles, became heiress to the manor of Marylebone, recently acquired by her father the Duke of Newcastle for £17,000. Within two years, she herself was acquired. She and her manorial fields were married to Edward, son of Robert Harley, 1st Earl of Oxford and Prime Minister to Queen Anne. This union produced just one child, a daughter, Margaret Cavendish Harley, who would also inherit the manor. Margaret's prodigious wealth attracted the attention of the Dutch diplomat, Hans Willem Bentinck, whose fame rested on his negotiation of the royal marriage of William of Orange to Princess Mary. He was showered with honours and an estate in Soho. But no matrimonial diplomacy stood him in better stead than that between his own grandson and Margaret Harley. The boy became the 2nd Duke of Portland and 'the handsomest man in England'. The manor of Marylebone became the Portland estate (now de Walden by female descent). To this day, its streets commemorate the Bentinck family's names, titles and country villages and estates: Portland, Harley, Wimpole, Welbeck, Holles, Vere. Landowners visiting London for the season, or eventually coming there to live, did not like to forget their country origins. Paris street names commemorate politicians and generals. Those in London record the country properties of the nobility and gentry.

To the south, the scientist and antiquarian Sir Hans Sloane had bought the Manor of Chelsea in 1712, but was no more successful than his fellow landowners in producing sons. His daughter Elizabeth was soon snapped up together with the east part of the manor by a Welshman, Cadogan of Oakley, whose family still owns most of the estate. North of the City, Elizabeth Spencer, heiress to the manors of Clerkenwell and Canonbury, was luckier. She was literally stolen, carried off in a basket by the dashing but penniless Lord Compton of Compton Wynyates. It was the most profitable elopement in London's history. The Northampton estate is still there as proof.

None of these women matched in prospects the 7-month-old child whose father, a City clerk named Alexander Davies, was felled by the plague of 1665. Davies had inherited what seemed little more than farm and swamp land near Westminster as his portion of the estate of his uncle by marriage, the Jacobean lawyer Hugh Audley. Alexander died intestate and his estate went, one-third to his 21-year-old wife Mary for her lifetime, and the rest including the manor of Ebury to his baby of the same name. The property stretched from the old Oxford road (now Oxford Street) in the north, down between the Westbourne and Tybourne streams to the Thames at Millbank. Only the old bailiwick of St James's, including what is now southern Mayfair, intruded on this large tract of land.

Five years after Alexander's death, a visitor to Hyde Park would have seen Restoration London in its prime. The City of London was fast rebuilding after the Great Fire but already developers had turned their attention to the fields north of the Court at St James's. A new West End was springing up round St James's Square, eager to challenge the other capitals of Europe as a centre of style and ostentation. Thirty years had passed since the Star Chamber had ordered the nobility and gentry back to their country estates lest they 'become unserviceable, and draw their money from the country and spend it in the City in excessive apparel'. London was again the hub of the nation. It was a snobbish society, but the snobbishness was of the newly arrived.

Nowhere was this confidence more on parade than at the Sunday promenades along the drives west of the city, notably the Ring (near today's Hyde Park Corner). North and south of these drives lay the most desirable land of all, that of Mary Davies's Ebury manor. It was towards Ebury that rows of houses were marching west from the City of Westminster. Ebury was the city's outer bailey. Its agricultural rents were already rising. Alexander was drawing £1,300 a year from them at the time of his death. He and his young wife had already moved from humble Southampton Buildings in Gray's Inn Road to a house in Millbank by the Lambeth horse ferry. There they engaged in a modest speculation, Alexander buying land from his brother and hoping to build riverside houses upstream of Westminster. Others, including Alexander's young widow, began to see wider opportunities in the estate.

Even by the extravagant standards of the Ring, one sight in 1670 would have turned all eyes. It was that of the infant Mary, now 5 years old, well-dressed, in a coach drawn by six horses and attended by servants and an aunt. She had no title nor did she live in any of the splendid town houses of Piccadilly. As the afternoon wore on, her coach did not rattle east towards the City, but turned south past Goring House (site of the present Buckingham Palace) along muddy tracks towards the Thames. There she lived a lonely life, guarded by her young mother and her aunt like a porcelain doll crammed with gold.

Rarely has greed been more blatantly on display than in Mary's treatment by her mother in the years following her father's death. The mother promptly remarried. Her new husband was John Tregonwell, a country gentleman and Member of Parliament from Dorset. They found themselves facing prolonged litigation over Alexander's uncompleted Millbank speculation and other relics of his estate. The story of this litigation, a classic of London history, was researched and published in 1921 by the Grosvenor Estate historian, Charles Gatty. Nothing in Gatty's tale is more astonishing than the cool-headedness with which the new Mrs Tregonwell, still in her early twenties, set about exploiting her prize asset. The character of London's West End is her memorial.

It was not uncommon for parents to sell their daughters for

cash where a substantial inheritance was involved. Where there is demand and supply there is likely to be a price. For the manor of Ebury, whether embodied in animate or inanimate form, that price was bound to be high. And it would be higher the longer the asset could be held in a rising market. We have no record of Mary Tregonwell suffering from any scruple on her daughter's behalf, but her correspondence shows a remarkable head for the business. Young Mary did not receive much serious education; her later correspondence shows an unsteady command of grammar and an awareness of her lack of accomplishment. Little consideration appears to have been given by her mother to her future happiness. Mrs Tregonwell wished to see her daughter placed in a rank appropriate to her wealth, and at a price that would enable the Tregonwells to pay off the debts on the Millbank speculations.

Mary was put in the care of her aunt, Mrs Mason, who was to act as her governess and be paid 'for her pains'. She was given three servants to wait on her and a coach and six to parade her in the park, unusual ostentation for a small girl. Her guardians were warned by mother and stepfather that nothing must happen to her and nobody be allowed to approach her until the moment was judged right to put her on to the market. Mrs Tregonwell later wrote, 'All things were carried on with the air of greatness answerable to the fortune she was supposed to have.' Her biographer, Gatty, put it differently: 'The free gaiety of her childhood had this dark shadow thrown across it. Every precaution had to be taken lest she should be stolen.'

In December 1672, when Mary was not yet 8, Mrs Tregonwell decided her asset was approaching maturity. The Lord Lieutenant of Ireland, Lord Berkeley of Stratton, was in town. He was blessed with a great name, a position at court, a mansion in Piccadilly and the ownership of Hay Hill farm behind it. By a series of now obscure negotiations, Mrs Tregonwell agreed to marry her daughter to Berkeley's 10-year-old son Charles. This was a fine match. In addition to his titles and status, Berkeley offered the marriage of the Hay Hill property to the Ebury holdings, neatly filling most of the gap between the north and south parts of the manor. This territorial aggrandizement must have appealed to Lord Berkeley, who can have had no other interest in the deal. Like Mrs Tregonwell, he was bartering status for wealth.

Mrs Tregonwell's terms were tough. She demanded £5,000 payable to her immediately in cash. This she intended to use to pay off her debts at Millbank. In addition there would be £3,000 in land settled on Charles and Mary as part of the marriage contract. Lord Berkeley's seniority was apparently of no account. Mrs Tregonwell, still just 28, was calling the tune. Lord Berkeley duly raised the £5,000 and paid it to her. The receipt for it rests in the Grosvenor archives. But he had trouble finding the £3,000 in land, indeed he could not do so. Mrs Tregonwell was not to be trifled with and promptly called off the deal. The unfortunate Charles Berkeley died ten years later in command of a ship at sea. What might have been a drastic new direction in the development of Mayfair was forestalled. The Berkeleys had to confine their development to Hay Hill, Berkeley and Stratton Streets and their eponymous square.

The Tregonwells now had to refund the £5,000 that they had already spent clearing the Millbank debts. The market appears to have remained hot, but four years passed before another deal was struck. Mrs Tregonwell chose, so she later wrote, 'among the many offers that were made' and decided on a 20-year-old baronet from Cheshire named Sir Thomas Grosvenor. She declared that his 'circumstance, family and character appeared to be most suitable and accordingly a treaty was entered into and he and his friends had the matter laid before them and six weeks given them to consider of it'. Grosvenor's many qualities included a kindly temperament, sorely tried in the years ahead, and a substantial income from his Cheshire properties, where he had just commenced the rebuilding of his family's home at Eaton. He was not poor, was already mature and the attractions of a child bride might seem obscure. Yet Mrs Tregonwell offered him an estate near London, close to the Court and to Parliament, where Grosvenor already had political ambitions. We must assume that the prospect was sufficiently appealing.

The contract was drawn up and agreed. Sir Thomas had to pay dearly for his prize. Mary was only 12, eight years his junior, and would remain in London until her fifteenth birthday. He had to make an allowance of £500 a year towards her upkeep. A further £50 was for Mrs Mason, the governess, and £5,000 plus £1,500 in interest was to be paid direct to Lord Berkeley in settlement of the previous abortive deal. Thus Mrs Tregonwell both cleared her own estate of debt and assured her daughter of a title when still in her minority. The marriage duly took place at St Clement Danes in the Strand on 10 October 1677. We have no record of how Mary performed at the ceremony or of her presumed bewilderment at the proceedings. It was not until 1680 that she finally travelled north with her husband to become mistress of Eaton Hall, then a simple house but later to be rebuilt by Waterhouse as a Gothic palace (now demolished). She became mistress also of the Grosvenors' Cheshire estate. Half a century later its names were to become famous back at Ebury: villages such as Belgrave, Eccleston, Kinnerton, Churton, Halkin and the city of Chester itself, names now synonymous with residential opulence.

The story of Mary Davies was not to end there. The impact on the young girl of her cosseted upbringing can only be imagined. Once installed at Eaton she was subject to fits of temperament that tried her husband's love and patience. Gatty quotes a letter from him to her, 'Your unkindness to me sometimes strikes me to the heart and you do not know the hurt it doth me . . . If you value my life you may preserve it, and leave those contradictions that you may think little, and those passionate concerns and rash words.' Such outpourings were to no avail. Mary, still a teenager, found companionship in the local Roman Catholic community. Among her friends was one William Massey, five years her senior and from a longstanding Catholic family. With Sir Thomas often in London, Mary, pregnant with three boys in succession, found these pious, still ostracized people a source of comfort. Before she was 20 she appears to have been admitted to the Catholic faith. Her old home at Millbank in London was let to a prominent Catholic, the 2nd Earl of Peterborough.

These were not propitious times for the head of a great family to flirt with Catholicism. The papacy was still seen as a threat to the constitution and 'popish plots' were a perpetual source of populist paranoia. The Grosvenors were a long-established Protestant family and Sir Thomas at the age of 24 had been returned as the local Member of Parliament. His wife's rumoured conversion may at first have been no more than an embarrassment, but it soon gave rise to official concern. A military report from Chester warned that 'frequent and great meetings of Roman Catholics every week at Sir Thomas Grosvenor's have occasioned his neighbours to complain of him . . . There should be no hesitation in the magistrates to order their arrest or for the military power to assist.' Worse was to come. In 1697 Mary began to show the first signs of a mental illness that worsened throughout the rest of her life. For Sir Thomas the anguish did not last long. In 1700 he fell ill and died, leaving Mary as head of the family with three boys and a girl. She had little of the level-headedness that had served her mother so well in a similar crisis. Shortly before his death, Sir Thomas took the precaution of entrusting the 'sole tuition and guardianship' of his children to trustees. To Mary he left the use of Eaton only until his eldest son should marry, together with his coach and horses. Thus was Alexander Davies' inheritance disposed.

Dame Mary, as now titled, was unstable and surrounded by Catholic associates in Cheshire of whose good intentions and advice she was not a sound judge. The Grosvenor trustees considered getting her certified as a lunatic, but were deterred by the damage this might do to the prospects of her eldest boy, Sir Richard, the new baronet. They must soon have regretted their leniency. Within two months of her husband's funeral and the birth of their last child, Mary announced that she intended to travel to the Continent in the company of her new Catholic chaplain and close friend, a Benedictine monk named Father Fenwick. After many attempts by friends to dissuade her, she set out from Eaton for Grosvenor House in London, then still situated on the old Davies land on Millbank. It was during this visit that she was painted by Michael Dahl: the only portrayal we have of her, a round-faced rather haughty woman of 35, but still youthful and attractive.

In London Fenwick gathered round her a small party and left for Paris and Rome. Paris at the time was the haunt of expatriate English Catholics who had fled with James II in 1688. To the Grosvenors, it was as if Mary had gone over to the enemy. The arrival of so wealthy a lady in Paris was naturally the cause of

8

much attention but the visit soon degenerated into a shambles. At one stage, Mary tried to send one of her maids to a French nunnery. Her travelling companion, Mrs Turnour, who was Fenwick's sister, returned to London. Mary did eventually reach Rome, accompanied by the ubiquitous Fenwick, but returned unwell to Paris in June 1701. What happened next is a mystery. Mary was incarcerated in the Hôtel Castile, being treated with a mixture of emetics, opium pills and constant bleeding. She was at the same time visited by another member of the Fenwick family, the chaplain's elder brother, Edward, who had met her briefly during her stopover in London. One Saturday night, with Mary dangerously ill, Edward Fenwick announced to his Paris friends that he and Lady Grosvenor were now man and wife, his brother having performed the ceremony the previous night.

The news plunged the Grosvenor family into turmoil. It marked the beginning of a series of court cases in London and Paris, as Fenwick and his friends sought the fruits of their conspiracy. With such wealth at stake, the law took full advantage of them. Mary returned desperate to London where she bitterly protested at her 'ill usage'. As for the wedding, she wrote to the Grosvenors' London agent, Mr Andrews, that 'I positively deny it and so will swear, and shall never own any such thing, it being absolutely false; for I never saw books, or heard marriage words, nor said any.' Fenwick was undeterred. He returned from Paris and presented himself in London to demand his conjugal rights. Mary's family removed her from London to Cheshire.

More seriously, Fenwick proceeded round the London properties demanding that the former Davies tenants now pay rent to him and not to the Grosvenor agent. Any doubt over the destination of rents was devastating both to the estate's income and to confidence in the future of what would in the short term be highly speculative development of the Ebury fields. Fenwick showed himself shrewd and unscrupulous. He lodged pleas before both the ecclesiastical and the secular courts for the recognition of his marriage. He threatened to eject any tenants not paying him rent and, as the matter was *sub judice*, the Court of Chancery had to insist that all rents on Grosvenor's London property be paid to the court until the matter was settled.

Those who marvel at the capacity of British law to create injustice by means of delay need look no further than *Fenwick* v. *Grosvenor*. For five years the fate of the largest and potentially most profitable slice of West London hung in the balance. Lawyers fumbled and feuded. They drew huge fees and showed little concern for any distress to the parties concerned. In effect they aided and abetted a fraud. Reading the accounts of the case, I do not doubt that Fenwick would have succeeded had Sir Thomas not chosen as his son's trustees men fiercely loyal to his family, Sir Richard Middleton and Thomas and Francis Cholmondeley. Within a year they had succeeded in getting Fenwick committed to prison in Paris for the felony of coercing a woman into marriage. (Fenwick might have pleaded that he was not the first to have done this to Mary Davies.) In France at the time this was a capital offence. But Fenwick was lucky. That year war broke out between France and Britain and he was able to bribe his way out of the Little Châtelet prison and make his way back to London.

Here he renewed his suits. A year later, in 1703, legal authorities more leisurely than those in France brought the case to a hearing before the Queen's Bench Division in Westminster Hall. An extraordinary series of witnesses to the 'marriage' were called by Fenwick. The jury found in his favour, that a wedding had indeed taken place that night in Paris. At the same time, Middleton and Cholmondeley were contesting Fenwick's suit in the Ecclesiastical Court of Delegates, a body less sympathetic to the plottings of a group of Catholics. Speed was not a strength of this court either. At least it was sure. Two years later, in 1705, the Church found in Mary's favour, concluding that the Paris marriage was null and void and effectively overturning the Queen's Bench decision. It is hard to imagine what would have happened to Mayfair and Belgravia had the decision gone the other way.

During this whole time, Mary had been kept a virtual prisoner at Eaton and Vale Royal, the Cholmondeley home. She grew increasingly demented with the passage of time, her mind plagued by memories of that dreadful Paris visit. She would boast of her friends in high places in the Church. Her mother, Mrs Tregonwell, was naturally still active. But her concern was less with her daughter's health or happiness than with ensuring that, whatever happened to the Grosvenor estate, her 'one-third for life' of the Davies property was kept distinct from the litigation. The determined old lady lived on in her house on Millbank, dying there in 1717.

Her daughter, Dame Mary, survived in the care of friends until her death in 1730, by which time her sons had begun to carry out their father's ambition for Ebury, commencing with Grosvenor Square in 1725. The development, which continued for a century and a half, was to cover the whole of north Mayfair, Belgravia and the low-lying marshes of Pimlico. It made the descendants of Mary Davies the biggest landowners in London. Combined with their provincial and overseas estates, the Dukes of Westminster, as they later became, amassed one of the largest private fortunes in Britain. Their only substantial disposal was of the Pimlico estate, between Victoria Station and the river, to pay death duties in the 1950s.

The Grosvenors acted as sound custodians of the manor of Ebury. They employed good developers and created some of the finest urban architecture in the world. Not only were they rich, but the care with which they tended their urban leases ensured that most of their tenants were rich also. The boundaries of the Grosvenor Estate must encompass more spending power than any other freehold in the world. Grosvenor leases were rigorously enforced. Yet the estate was prominent in the late nineteenth century in granting land to the Peabody and other working-class housing charities, much of whose work survives there to this day. The family's power over the lives of ordinary Londoners was extraordinary, but as on all London estates it could be exerted only as long as development was prudent and market forces respected. Many West London estates showed little respect for either and suffered, for instance that of the Church Commissioners in Bayswater and the Ladbroke family in Notting Hill.

Perhaps all good things come to an end. The Major government's 1993 Housing and Urban Development Act was supposedly aimed at extending home-ownership and releasing established tenants from the bondage of bad landlordism. If a few noble babies were tossed out with the bathwater, so be it. If the great estates of London were undone, too bad. Local planning authorities would in future be responsible for conservation and good husbandry. Few questioned that the Act was put into the 1992 Conservative manifesto in an attempt to win votes in London marginal seats. No great social evil was being rectified. Politicians were simply acting in furtherance of their personal advantage.

I can only reflect that life was ever thus. Sir Thomas Grosvenor's original bargain was to the same purpose. Five thousand pounds plus interest brought him political position and wealth. History has come full circle. If the London estates are now to change irrevocably, we can only admire the estate that the Grosvenors built on such a mercenary foundation, and sympathize with the little girl who was so patently its victim.

2

THE GREAT BANKRUPTS

LONDONERS ARE not good at receiving bad news. In early 1524 soothsayers told them the city had become so squalid and venal that the Thames would rise up and flood it in punishment. Ten thousand properties would be submerged. The terrible date was predicted to be 1 February. On that day a vast throng, rich and poor, some said half the population of the city, fled to the high ground of Hampstead and Harrow. Monks in the latter fortified their house against the mob. The crowd spent a bleak night in the open. The following day they trooped back home, cursing the pundits as they went.

We have less faith in forecasters nowadays. Yet ever since Cobbett castigated the Great Wen – indeed long before him – apocalyptic language has been part and parcel of living in the city. London is perpetually 'in crisis'. It is eternally grinding to a halt, seizing up, on the point of collapse. The economy is faltering, homelessness soaring, public services in terminal decline. The recession of the early 1990s was no different. The media wailed, studies were commissioned, think-tanks set up. Paris was 'about to take over from London' as commercial capital of Europe, so was Frankfurt and Brussels and even Milan. Domestic house prices, like office property, had no sooner ceased being in a vicious upward spiral than

13

they were in a no less vicious downward one. Good news was out of fashion.

House prices in 1992 certainly fell steeply, by over a quarter, for the first time in most Londoners' living memory. Unemployment figures suggested that parts of Greater London were in a deeper recession than anywhere in Britain other than the industrial north. Crime figures seemed on a remorseless upward trend. Statistics on commercial property early in the year indicated that as much as a fifth of the central business district was available for letting. Thoroughfares such as London Wall and Upper and Lower Thames Street looked festive as owners decked them in banners proclaiming the 'unbeatable value' of the space within. There were To Let signs on all sides. The Canary Wharf development on the Isle of Dogs, including the highest office tower in Europe, went into receivership, as did the fifteen largest East London commercial and residential projects. From Butler's Wharf through Tobacco Dock to Burrell's Wharf, the city was a stage set for a disaster film.

London's economic ups and downs have often been severe. They are mostly indicated by surges in building activity, accompanied by political pressure to curb it. Such curbs tend to be so belated that controls bite only when the boom has spent its force. They thereby exacerbate the next downturn. This fuels recession and encourages the prediction that London is finished as a vibrant national capital. I remember Sir John Betjeman saying in the depths of the mid-1970s recession that London's prospects were so poor that he would soon be able to graze sheep on Southwark Bridge. Ten years later, property developers were fighting each other like Romans and Tuscans at each end of this same bridge – to erect buildings that were soon lying empty. A cycle is a cycle. Every drought ends in rain. As what goes up must come down, so what goes down must come up.

What determines the turning of a London property cycle remains obscure. We seem baffled by the forces that shift the city economy into forward gear, enabling it to bounce back from each slump with renewed vigour. My favourite barometer of London prosperity is building activity. It is the easiest to observe. Cranes, hoardings, building sites, To Let signs tell stories no statistic can distort. What a contractor puts up stays up until replaced. How it is occupied and by whom cannot be concealed. The builders in each cycle leave their high-water mark, their geological layer, detectable in the architecture. The 'town improvement' boom of the 1770s left the Georgian estates of Bloomsbury, Marylebone and Chelsea, and was brought to an end by the Napoleonic wars. The post-Waterloo boom of the 1820s left Regency Belgravia, Regent's Park, Bayswater. It ended in the stock market crash of 1825. A resurgence at the end of the 1830s created Pimlico, Islington and St John's Wood, ending in the crash of 1847. The Great Exhibition lifted the city out of the 1850s slump and left north and south Kensington and the first railway suburbs. It coated North, West and much of South London in Italianate mansions and stucco façades. This boom was sustained by the outward expansion of public transport and the advent of the Underground. A grey sea of working-class housing spread between the white cliffs of stucco. It made London the biggest metropolis in Europe, and ended in the slump of the 1880s.

Further expansions occurred in the Edwardian period and in the suburban 'gold rush' of the 1930s, in Metroland and Finchley, in bypass Tudor and Roadhouse Georgian. In twenty years, London more than doubled its built-up area. After the Second World War, upturns occurred with the end of building controls in the 1950s and in the property boom of the late 1960s and early '70s. The latter left the dirtiest of tidemarks, the government offices of Victoria Street and Marsham Street; the Seifert hotels that dot the West London skyline; the 'planning gain' towers over new road junctions at Euston, Centre Point and near Victoria. The most recent upturn, boosted by the Lawson boom of the mid-1980s, saw one of the wildest cycles of all. The unimaginable happened: London suffered a brief shortage of architects.

These booms seem to drift out of public memory in time of recession, just as recession is forgotten by developers in time of boom. Through good and bad periods alike, an ingrained urban pessimism prevails. The public moans about overcrowding and congestion when the market is up. It moans about bankruptcy and shabbiness when the market is down. Cities appear to be treated as necessary evils. Just as we seek them, often desperately, when

15

young so we yearn to flee them as we grow older. Maturity seems to involve a turning away from the city, from its rootlessness, its risks, its novelty, its opportunity. To be rude about London is taken as a sign of sanity. London is for those without a stake in any sort of country.

I intend to take a leaf from the Red Queen's book. It was, she said, a poor sort of memory that only works backwards. Let us look at London's past and try to remember forwards. The litmus test for the end of a London economic cycle is simple, it is the appearance over the horizon of that shadowy character, the bankrupt developer. He usually comes not in single spies but in battalions. The most splendid of all was John Nash, developer by appointment to the Prince Regent, later George IV. His struggle in the 1820s to develop Regent Street and Regent's Park makes today's travails on the Isle of Dogs seem small beer. Only a handful of Nash's fifty Regent's Park villas were ever built, each to be enclosed by its own private landscape from which the others would be invisible. The contractor of the planned double circus at the top of Portland Place went bankrupt with just half of one circus finished, the now semi-circular Park Crescent.

To the south, in Regent Street itself, Nash had to abandon his unified design because he could not sell all the sites at one time and to one pattern. This piecemeal development made easier the sad demolition and redevelopment of the street when the leases ran out in the first quarter of this century. Nash himself took on the risk of building the Quadrant by Piccadilly Circus, as sub-developers went bankrupt beneath him. He finally had to persuade the bricklayers to take shares in the houses they were building instead of cash. That bankrupted still more.

Nash was not just overambitious. He was unlucky. With the crash of 1825, he ran out of building cycle. The proposed triumphal way from Trafalgar Square north through Soho to the present British Museum, to match Regent's Street, got no further than the West Strand Improvements, now standing with its 'pepper pots' opposite Charing Cross. Nor was the apparent wealth of a development any protection against collapse, if anything the reverse. The richer the prospects, the more likely appears to have been bankruptcy. Of the three men selected by the Grosvenor Estate in the

1820s to develop the fields of the old manor of Ebury in Belgravia – Smith, Cundy and Cubitt – only the redoubtable Cubitt survived one building cycle. In Chester Square, Cundy cramped his houses tight round a small patch of grass, hardly meriting the term square, completing them just before he went broke. Millionaires and former prime ministers now occupy his modest terraces.

Even Cubitt had his troubles. He built what turned out to be the Canary Wharf of his day at Albert Gate on Knightsbridge: the two largest private houses yet constructed in London. They were equipped with such gadgets as hoists and even a passenger lift. They stood empty for years. Londoners dubbed them Malta and Gibraltar as they would 'never be taken'. The east block eventually went to Hudson 'the railway king', and doubtless contributed to his own financial ruin. It is now the French Embassy. Long may it prosper as such. When Cubitt reached the marshy land of Pimlico he had an even harder time. Extensive drainage and sewerage were necessary, the most advanced in the world at that time. But the market was turning and Pimlico shows it. Unlike Belgravia, Pimlico has a pub on every corner, sign of Cubitt's concern to keep his builders lubricated and on the job for fear of buyers vanishing before completion. Cubitt at least kept shops and services to the fringes of his estate. When the South Coast railway came to Victoria his successors were able to insist that its route from the river be roofed to keep the soot off Belgravia's washing, and rubber dampers be inserted beneath the rail sleepers. No such concern for the slumber of residents was noticeable at Paddington or Euston. Walk these streets today and you can see London's economic history writ on every façade.

Further west, another salubrious neighbourhood took a quarter-century to develop. In the 1830s the Crown Commissioners decided to erect the most extravagant avenue in Europe in the grounds of Kensington Palace, a fit neighbour for a royal palace. London estates, however, never bore risk on their own behalf. Their interest was in farming ground rents, usually on 99-year leases, not in gambling on property. For six years the Commissioners sought a developer for Kensington Palace Gardens. Not until 1844 did they find one named Blashfield to take the first twenty sites. Within three years, he was declared insolvent with not one house built.

The Commissioners auctioned his plots but found few takers. Development did not start until the next boom in the late 1850s. By then London's architecture had become more florid and spectacular. The avenue was not completed until the early twentieth century. Once nicknamed Millionaires' Row, Kensington Palace Gardens is now almost all embassy residences. The taxpayers of the world are the new rich.

The delay in developing this estate had one great benefit. Nash's Crown leases on Regent Street fell due, and thus came up for redevelopment, in the first half of this century. This was before the advent of historic buildings control and much of Nash's architecture was destroyed. Most of Georgian Mayfair and Park Lane was likewise doomed. The Kensington leases, like Cubitt's Belgravia ones, did not fall due until the 1950s and 1960s, by when control was in place. These terraces and squares survived lease renewal and remain among the glories of London.

Surviving too are the products of my favourite London bankrupts in Notting Hill. In the 1820s, old James Ladbroke attempted to develop what is now Ladbroke Square, but he fell foul of the Great Crash of '25. A few dejected villas were erected round a large circus, in the style of Regent's Park. They stood unoccupied and the circus was briefly turned over to horse racing, known as the Hippodrome. The upturn of the 1840s saw developers turning covetous eyes north-westwards. Two men, Duncan and Connop, took leases from Ladbroke and began work near the old Hippodrome. They were to go bankrupt within five years. Their Ladbroke interests were surrendered to various City creditors who felt, like most City men, that where mere fools had trod they need not fear failure. One of them, a man named Richard Roy, was to turn the fields of Notting Hill into the property gold rush of his age. Everybody wanted in. Country parsons, the widows of Anglo-Indian grandees, the unsuspecting aristocrats of Trollope's *The Way We Live Now*, all treated the Ladbroke estate like an Argentinian railway speculation. It proved even more risky. Roy did not last long but he at least built some houses before retreating to lick his wounds. Lansdowne Road and Lansdowne Walk are his monuments.

North and east of Roy's speculation lay the Portobello and

Notting Hill portions of the estate. Here a clergyman, Samuel Walker, inherited and spent on building work a quarter of a million pounds. He lasted just four years. With builders collapsing around him, and sometimes buildings too, he put the estate into trusteeship. Farther north, a man named Pocock took on the ruins of the old Westbourne Park estate, spent his fortune on it and died worth just £9,000. The one man to make money in Notting Hill seems to have been a colourful character named Blake. He arrived in the neighbourhood with qualifications more useful than any skill in finance or architecture. He was an indigo planter and sugar dealer from Calcutta. He wandered the brickfields of Notting Hill picking up everyone else's bankrupt leases. He even managed to survive the 1850s slump. The shrewd developer knows that fortunes are built not in good times but in bad ones.

Most of Notting Hill took over a century to acquire the middle-class status its ground landlord had envisaged for it. Desperate developers even changed the area's name, passing it off as North Kensington. It languished for decades. Ladbroke Gardens was known as Coffin Row because of its half-built gap-toothed houses. Even in the booming 1860s the district was still a ghost town. It was described by *Building News* as 'a graveyard of buried hopes . . . the melancholy vestiges of the wreck are not yet cleared away: naked carcasses, crumbling decorations, fractured walls, slimy cement. All who touch them lose heart and money by the venture.'

When buildings were taken, they swiftly went 'down market' into multi-occupation and dereliction, home of the poorest of the city's poor. This was a land of brickmakers and potters, of Irish and then West Indian immigrants. Most of its streets and gardens stayed that way until the leases fell due in the 1960s. Then the northern parts of Notting Hill saw speculative redevelopment at its most cruel, 'winkling', evictions, homelessness and crime. The district's most notorious operator, Rachman, even gave his name to an -ism, gracing as Rachmanism a process of renewal as old as cities themselves. It took the Ladbroke estate not one building cycle or even two to recover from the excesses that attended its birth. It took a hundred years of bankruptcy and anguish.

Such scenes of boom and bust are not merely common in cities, they are the norm. In the case of London, free of walls and

battlements since the Middle Ages, development has moved out-
wards not in ripples but in tidal waves, ebbing and flowing. These
waves always had a political undertow. In 1580 Elizabeth I banned
all new building and even multi-occupation within three miles of
the centre of London. This proved counter-productive. Development did not stop but was jerry-built, since anything put up might
have to be pulled down overnight. Market forces were more
powerful than planners. These forces spread the city out over the
fields of Middlesex. From market gardening to brickmaking to
migrant squatting to terraced housing, the sequence that inspired
Dickens in *Dombey and Son* and *Our Mutual Friend* surged on
with only an occasional pause.

This open market showed signs of what economists call a hog
cycle. In good times developers rushed in, confident that they could
find a demand for their building in advance of any downturn in
the cycle. The lag between planning, building and letting naturally
led to a chronic oversupply. This surplus was bound to exacerbate
and thus prolong the subsequent downturn. Although wars and
other factors have accelerated or delayed the cycle, the London
property market has boomed and slumped roughly every two
decades since the Battle of Waterloo.

The experience of the past quarter-century shows that even the
world's most sophisticated planning machine – once London's
boast – is incapable of ironing out the peaks and troughs in the
property market. At the height of the last boom, in the mid-1980s,
planners in the City of London were offering office permissions
with abandon. They were told by their political masters that the
City had to compete with the no less reckless expansion of commercial property in Docklands. Far from evening out the boom/slump
cycle as planning ought to do, this rivalry exaggerated the 1980s
boom and made far worse the 1990s slump. This was not even
laissez-faire: it was anti-planning. Westminster City Council, to its
credit, was more restrained. It sought at this time to convert office
premises in Mayfair back to housing. This was sound conservation,
sound planning and sound commerce too. I can think of no better
case for a strategic planning authority than the overdevelopment
of the City and East London in the late 1980s.

London in the early 1990s behaved as London always does during a recession. It pondered the downturn and gloomily concluded, 'Ah, but this one is different, this one is terminal.' Previous downturns were mere pauses. Now London's economy was declining so fast as to be 'out of control'. Nothing could ever fill the empty acres of the Isle of Dogs or the Royal Docks. The City Airport would never survive. London employment peaked in the early 1960s and recovered only slightly in the late 1980s, when the rest of the south-east was booming. New employment was at what statisticians call an all-time low. Even bankers, doctors and lawyers were facing redundancy. Who knows but planners might be next.

History says this had to be rubbish. London's property market has never yet 'collapsed'. Markets only collapse if they are closed down, and even then they find ways of bubbling up again. The London property market has always been in rude health, doing what markets are supposed to do: fixing prices to bring demand and supply into equilibrium. In the late 1980s the market was certainly dazed, since its participants were ignoring the lesson of markets past. By 1990, the market had recovered its poise. Within two years it had slashed office rents by half and it went on slashing them. House prices from Kensington across central London to Tower Hamlets were down between 15 and 20 per cent on the year and falling. House prices in Docklands halved in the same two years.

One consequence was that the outmigration of offices almost stopped: a good thing in a recession but still being encouraged by government even when recession loomed. In 1991 only 14 substantial employers left the capital, compared with over 45 in 1990. Outmigration had virtually ceased in 1993. The devaluation of the pound brought buoyancy back to prices in the housing and office sectors; foreigners proved less susceptible to London gloom. For a time buyers were able to get repossessed London flats at auction and bankruptcy sales for as little as £15,000. Such repossessions, like bankruptcies, are a sign of a flexible property market and are the essential precondition for recovery, harrowing though they may be for those concerned.

London cannot fail to revive. Its industries are what they have always been, growth ones: government, politics, the law, banking and financial management, health and education, tourism and leisure, the arts and sport. These are activities much despised by left-wing economists, who believe that real cities are built on manufacturing. There has always been some manufacturing in the capital, but London has not depended on it. The city's assets are hard to quantify. They include its historic status as capital, its old buildings, its artistic pre-eminence, the world dominance of the English language. All give the place a magnetic appeal for the young, the rich and the poor. None of these assets is likely to decay or relocate far from the capital. I recently noted a list of potential tenants for a bankrupt development in Docklands. They included a Japanese bank, an American university, a British film maker, a government department and London Transport. You could hardly ask for a more typical spread of London activities.

In no world capital city are public administration and the professions in long-term decline. Nobody has ever managed to cut the number of bureaucrats employed in central and local public services. Tourism and its related industries of catering, hotels and the arts are certainly vulnerable to trade cycles but are on a long-term upward trend. The English language keeps London a natural focus for Europe's banking and finance and for education, publishing and the media. All these activities have economic multiplier effects. One Third World embassy has been estimated to keep a hundred Londoners gainfully employed, in everything from car repairs through language lessons to flower arrangement.

Many de-industrializing areas of England are said to be reliant on a small core of highly skilled and productive workers to sustain any new employment. By contrast, many of London's prevalent businesses demand a reserve of unskilled and semi-skilled labour. Dyos and Wolff in their study of employment in Victorian London drew attention to the importance of 'comers and goers' in the nineteenth-century economy. Irish labour sustained the construction industry. Cockneys moved back and forth between the winter gasworks and the summer hop fields of Kent. Tinkers, street sellers, carters, entertainers and domestic servants came and went in their hundreds of thousands. At the end of the century, additional swarms of economic refugees from East Europe and the Mediterranean descended on the rag and jewellery trades, then on the catering industry. Londoners moving up the economic ladder migrated to the suburbs, decrying the overcrowding, dirt and noise of the city as they left. But eager inward migrants were ready to take their places: waiters, kitchen workers, office cleaners, the mobile young from home and abroad. In a modern recession, secondary schools in the north of England find that their leavers still head south to work in kitchens or as nannies in the capital. Little has changed over a century.

New arrivals from overseas are no longer from familiar destinations, from Italy, Portugal and the white and non-white Commonwealth. Immigrants are the indicator-species of political turbulence around the globe. They have their own conduits and intelligence systems. They know where to find a house and a job. One day Filipino domestic servants arrive; the next, Polish construction gangs; then Nigerian single mothers; then refugees from Eritrea, Zaire, Somalia, Bosnia, whether the immigration authorities approve or not. They pour out of Terminal Three, are screened by a reception agency and disappear on to the Piccadilly Line, the Ellis Island of modern London.

This constant supply of new labour holds down wages and thus labour costs in the capital. The informal economy in which most immigrants participate is flexible. This is why capital cities and their service industries tend to survive recession better than those more dependent on manufacturing or on an indigenous, often unionized, workforce. Migrants fill the interstices of London development. When the suburban builders of Middlesex found a sluggish market in Golders Green and Finchley, they marketed to the upwardly mobile Jews of Brick Lane. Bangladeshis moved in to take the latter's place. When Tower Hamlets cleared the Chinese out of Limehouse in the 1960s, it coincided with the clearance of prostitutes out of Soho. The Chinese had colonized Limehouse fifty years before and simply moved four miles west to Gerrard Street. They are now part of London's heritage. When East London councils find decrepit tower blocks hard to let, Nigerian or Bangladeshi entrepreneurs buy up the rent books and fill the blocks with 'students' or single-parent families smuggled in from home. A Docklands developer may have dreamed of filling his Post-Modernist wharfside village with Big Bang yuppies. But any resident is better than none, and housing benefit money is at least secure. As Blake of Notting Hill would have said, the property market abhors a vacuum.

Of course each recovery has its defining characteristics, as did each preceding boom. More distant estates always take longer to recover from slump. Anachronistic buildings take longer to let. The Docklands boom of the late 1980s, fuelled by tax breaks, led to the overdevelopment of sites: too much office space set in too mean a landscape. This meant that the area was bound to take longer to climb back from bankruptcy. Who knows but it may take even longer than Notting Hill. Ladbroke's sub-contractors at least erected classical London houses. These have always proved adaptable, from multi-occupation to single-family use, from flats to offices to sweatshops and back to houses again. The fabric of the buildings can absorb each twist and turn in the property cycle. Canary Wharf or Thomas More Square or the Royal Mint or the Charing Cross building have no such flexibility. They were designed for the large computerized trading floors of the mid-1980s. They are about as adaptable as nuclear power stations.

Yet the lessons of Notting Hill can still be applied to Canary Wharf. The latter is no more than another chapter in the same story. An overambitious plan resulted in buildings unable to find tenants as the boom lost its force. The developer went bankrupt and the buildings reverted to the banks. By 1992 the essential precondition for recovery had taken place: an estate's initiators had spent and lost a fortune. The resulting buildings were unencumbered with debt and rents could be slashed to clear the market. The market was a tough one and may yet prove ruthless. Canary Wharf and most of its contemporaries are expensive buildings to occupy. The cost of maintenance was, at least at the time of completion, higher than the rent per square foot obtainable in the market. The Notting Hill message was clear: maintenance would have to deteriorate until demand was forthcoming at any price. Tenants must be found; any cash would be better than none. The odds must be on many of these blocks being mothballed – as was Centre Point in the 1960s – until some future upturn renders them lettable. They will be monuments to reckless government incentives and bad planning, but monuments too to London's way of

24

securing growth and renewal, two leaps forward and an occasional leap back.

I expect the 1990s will see an alarming phenomenon across much of central and East London, the squatting of empty office blocks and their slide into the black economy. A similar form of occupation has now overtaken many of the earlier residential blocks in the East End. Backstreet entrepreneurs with immigrant tenants and a certain amount of cash make better landlords, just, than a local council with neither cash nor willing tenants. Public-sector housing, put up with the best of intentions, has sunk back to the level of the worst of the private sector. An instructive parallel is the fate of many of the high-rise hotels of the Costa Brava. These emporia of working-class tourism were once packed with British visitors in search of Mediterranean sun, and not particular about the accommodation that came with it. The tourists have gone elsewhere, to Corfu, Majorca and Florida. The hotels have had to find a new market, and have done so in migrants from North Africa. The Costa Brava resorts have become teeming tenements filled with the poorest of immigrants, like the rookeries of Hong Kong or the *favelas* of Caracas.

Some architects in the East End have applied themselves to the possibility of converting large commercial office blocks to residential use. There seems little hope of turning 30,000 square feet of trading floor into middle-class homes. But there is no market more active than that in cheap housing. Even the most barren office block would offer shelter to the world's economic and political refugees. In the early 1990s, London was receiving unknown thousands from Somalia, Zaire and former Yugoslavia. They wanted no more than a roof. The plumbing could ride on a wing and a prayer. Should they descend on London's dozens of disused office blocks, I imagine they will regard them soon as home. Some future Rachman will have a tough job winkling such people out of them.

Nothing in the London property market should be a surprise. I am sure the Huguenot gentry who built the Georgian town houses of Spitalfields would not credit their present-day use, packed to the rafters with economic refugees from the fields of Bangladesh. The builders of Canary Wharf should prepare themselves to be no less amazed at who eventually turns up to occupy their marble halls. As long as any city keeps open the veins and arteries of its economy, it will recover. These arteries are those of traditional urban renewal, of buildings, the raw material of cities, responding to the changing demand of people for shelter. Cities may choose to be fastidious in time of plenty. They cannot be fastidious in recession. They must accept people as they come, any people, for the coming and going of people enables cities to live. Parts of London survive on a diet of social security payments, stolen cars, drugs and leather goods, just as other parts survive on the international bond market. Buildings must change to take account of these patterns of survival, sometimes surreptitiously, sometimes rampantly. Squatters may take over the rooms of company directors. Lichen may grow in the heating ducts of abandoned skyscrapers. Kestrels may nest on their roofs. The migrations that gave London Lombard Street, Old Jewry and Chinatown will bring Vietnam and Macedonia and Armenia to Wapping and Shadwell and Hoxton. Only when such colonies fail to materialize should London worry. A city composed only of goers, never comers, is a city that has lost its magnetic drive.

Urban history is the quietest of tutors. Its message is so often obscured by the city's din, by the ceaseless tramp of the new, the ugly and the exhilarating. But the message is there, hidden beneath busy streets and great buildings, beneath successive waves of optimism and pessimism. Tap on history's door and it will sit you down and tell you its story. In the life of cities there is no crisis, only birth, death and rebirth.

3

VENI, VIDI, VENTURI

I FIRST laid eyes on the embryo Sainsbury wing of the National Gallery in the glorious spring of 1987. The month was April and I had begun the morning with a walk over Waterloo Bridge to the Hayward Gallery on the South Bank. I have never liked this place. Here in London's Memorial to the Unknown Architect was an exhibition dedicated to the work of its aesthetic progenitor, Le Corbusier. His was a future that had not worked. If evidence was required, it was all around me in that concrete excrescence skulking on the bank of the river. By way of antidote, I walked upstream to the Tate Gallery to see James Stirling's Clore extension, which had opened the month before. The building was designed to house the Turner collection and nestled in friendly conversation with the Tate portico next door. Ten years before there had been a mighty battle to stop the Gallery pulling this portico down. Now the grand old man was secure. Next door, Stirling's walls, windows, triangles and arches were witty and colourful. They glowed fresh in the spring sunshine.

With spirits revived, I continued north to Trafalgar Square. Here I entered a city of columns: Nelson's Column, columns behind on Inigo Jones's Banqueting House, columns on Smirke's Canada House, columns on Baker's South Africa House, columns galore on Wilkins's National Gallery, columns on Gibbs's

27

St Martin-in-the-Fields. Only in the top left-hand corner was there a column-free gap. Here in 1984 the heirs of Le Corbusier had wanted to erect one of a number of contrasting designs as an extension of the National Gallery. They proposed boxes, blank walls or high-tech tubes and drums, the 'monstrous carbuncles' of Prince Charles's celebrated denunciation. The proposal had been dropped.

On display in the Gallery itself was yet another plan, a model of a £30m wing to house the collection of Early Renaissance paintings. The design was the work of Robert Venturi, a shy rather donnish professor from Philadelphia, assisted by his voluble and assertive wife, Denise Scott Brown. They were on hand to show visitors their work. She talked incessantly. He smiled meekly in the background, nervous of British architectural criticism, feared in America for its ferocity. He remarked that the British press 'takes, let us say, a more expressionist approach to architecture' than the American.

The designs were a triple triumph, of architecture, gallery design and implementation. The greatest of these was implementation. Ever since the site had been bombed in the Blitz, committees, lobbies and Gallery trustees had been campaigning to fill it with something other than a car park. Before the last war, Calouste Gulbenkian had promised to pay for an extension to the Gallery on the site, an offer withdrawn when the government declared this Anglophile benefactor an enemy alien in 1939. More attempts followed. An architectural competition in 1959 produced a concrete design that was howled down in the House of Commons. In 1981 a decision was made to go for a mixed commercial and gallery development, with offices paying for new exhibition space. This was seen as embodying the prevailing ideal of public- and private-sector partnership. The mixture was a failure: the 'carbuncle' design of architects Ahrends, Burton and Koralek. They had been hamstrung by the developers, Trafalgar House, a firm with a poor record of architectural patronage and eager for an office headquarters in such a prestigious location. The art of the Renaissance was consigned to a tenancy in the attic, and made to seem so.

Following yet another public outcry and the intervention of the Prince of Wales, the trustees found themselves back at square one.

At this point, the Sainsbury brothers stepped in. They said they were ready to put up all the money required to build an extension, untrammelled by commercial cross-subsidy. This was to be their show and their show alone. A team of assessors scoured the world for a suitable architect, with no more public consultation. Like Renaissance princes, the Sainsburys were paying the piper. They intended to call the tune, and fast. While the Venturis were not on the first shortlist, Denise Scott Brown's hustling eventually won them not only an interview but also the prize. Robert Venturi was, he said, 'the happiest architect in the world'.

When I saw it that April day the model was lit to look like a wedding cake. It floated on its pedestal, quite unlike the lumpen polystyrene blocks favoured by many architectural practices. Most noticeable, and controversial, was the exterior. Here Venturi had appeared to gather up all the columns in Trafalgar Square, put them in his quiver and fire them one by one at his façade. His language was the Corinthian of the National Gallery, carried over a short bridge and given a syncopated rhythm. His columns were first clustered, then spaced between false windows, then petered out altogether as the corner was turned towards Pall Mall. On this corner Venturi placed a final solitary column, attached to the blank wall. It looked back across the Square and thumbed its nose at the whole pompous assembly: 'You have had your say, now I am going to have fun.' Next Venturi had lifted up the skirt of his façade and revealed a sequence of coloured Egyptian columns on the ground floor, carrying the Portland stone wall round the back of the building. Venturi's love of eclecticism was gloriously on parade. Never have I seen the two great languages of Mediterranean architecture in such happy partnership.

The model attracted 70,000 visitors. The overwhelming majority of comments were favourable. Planning and heritage bodies reacted with equal pleasure. The Prince of Wales was induced to bless it as 'a building of which London can be proud'. The consensus was now to get on with it. The only serious discord came from the architectural critics, and some of this was vitriolic. (The Venturis' fears were more than justified.) The entire neo-Modernist lexicon of abuse was thrown at the design: pastiche, façadism, shallow, untruthful, cynical, unserious. The

Architectural Review dismissed the façade as 'a piece of picturesque mediocre slime'. The art critic Brian Sewell called it simply 'badly designed'. Gavin Stamp said it was 'a camp joke, pretentious architectural rubbish and an insult to London'. His *Independent* colleague, Henry Porter, found himself 'wondering at Venturi's sanity'. It was 'more post office than Post-Modern'. He was particularly offended by Venturi's Egyptian columns, describing them as 'like a pastel power station constructed in the Thirties'. This is the moment, said Porter, 'at which you know beyond all doubt that Robert Venturi is having you on'.

Venturi took this in relatively good part. He was happy to admit that aspects of his design were to be approached with a sense of humour. 'What was wrong with humour in architecture?' he asked. Why should British critics be shocked by fun? There were other more gentle criticisms. Some drew attention to the blankness of the side and rear façades, a defect Venturi partly corrected in execution, and to the blankness of the glass wall to the main staircase exterior (which he could not correct). The Chairman of the Royal Fine Art Commission, Lord St John of Fawsley, took exception to the 'austere mousehole' of the street entrance, a view I share but which Venturi vigorously rejected.

The Sainsburys were undaunted at the criticism. The building was widely liked and was going to happen. There was an end to it. With a new chairman, Lord Rothschild, a new director, Neil MacGregor, and two rich benefactors in the Sainburys (building) and John Paul Getty (acquisitions), the National Gallery was experiencing the smack of firm leadership. Walking round it at the time I sensed a new smartness in the attendants, almost a new bloom on the paintings themselves. It was four more years before the wing was completed, years in which the Venturis and the Gallery concealed its appearance behind thick curtains of netting. They reasonably felt that the next bite of the critical cherry should come when the work was completed and could be appreciated inside as well as out. On 9 July 1991 that moment came with the opening by the Queen.

The interior won and has continued to win almost universal praise. Only the ground and mezzanine floors were criticized for their mean proportions, constrained by the planning requirements of the site and by a desire to get the maximum height on the gallery floor. This floor is one of the London's most majestic architectural spaces. A grand staircase leads from the street entrance up into the daylight, giving views of Trafalgar Square on one side and, on the other, the incised names of Renaissance artists – Duccio, Piero, Mantegna, Bellini – to remind us of the splendours within. It is a palace wall within a palace. At the top, Venturi introduces us to a long vista, to the right penetrating the entire length of the National Gallery, to the left through a series of arches culminating in Cimabue's altarpiece, *The Incredulity of St Thomas*. Each arch in the gallery reflects the arch in the picture itself.

The interior spaces of the Sainsbury wing are attuned to the art they contain. Never has such meticulous attention been paid to the hanging of paintings. A complete mock-up of one room with copies of pictures on its walls was constructed at Shepperton film studios, so that every aspect could be tested and adjusted. Particular attention was paid to wall materials and colours – much criticized at the Clore Gallery. The fall of light from the roof openings was carefully monitored. Further models were constructed as the 'hang' was debated by the staff. In an elegant comment on the outcome of all this labour, the chairman Lord Rothschild remarked, 'I do not think, I'm afraid, that anything has gone very, very wrong.'

Here are none of the portentous chambers of the old National Gallery or the Louvre, nor the frigid classicism of the Metropolitan or Washington's National Gallery. All is seemliness. Arches, columns, stone courses, grey paintwork, ceiling lights, proportions, doorways, all are meant to be reminiscent of the spirit of Renaissance Italy. The reference is unmistakable yet not overpoweringly so. It is as if Venturi was seeking to recreate the same spatial volumes as surrounded the pictures in their original locations. Never, except perhaps at the Frick in New York, have I felt such correctness of proportion in a gallery. *The Times* art critic, Richard Cork, admired Venturi's 'imperturbability', the lack of a sense of strain in his design: 'His walls slope inwards before rising to clerestory windows, an ingenious device preventing the gallery height from becoming oppressively awesome . . . The emphasis throughout is on limpidity and absolute concentration.'

31

Where small altarpieces require intimacy, the architecture supplies it. Where, as in the Piero della Francesca room, one artist demands exclusive attention, the building responds. Where Raphael's great *Crucifixion* calls for a return to theatre, Venturi obliges with a crescendo of arches the length of the building. We weave our way from aisle to nave, from chancel to apse, from narthex to antechapel. Never does the building shout. I have returned time and again to these rooms, sometimes when they are deserted and calm, sometimes when they are filled with tourist hubbub. Already I find it hard to imagine the pictures hanging anywhere else or in any other manner. The art of Renaissance Italy and Northern Europe was meant for here, because here was meant for it. This is the greatest compliment that can be paid to architecture.

The passage of time has likewise settled Venturi's controversial façade into its context. It still leads the eye with a light-hearted skip and a jump out of Trafalgar Square into Pall Mall. I am still not reconciled to the doorway and I still find the ground floor unnecessarily subterranean. But these are quibbles. London has a new masterpiece. Venturi's building deserves to be seen as a turning point in London's post-Modern renaissance. There are bigger manifestations, such as Farrell's Charing Cross and Vauxhall developments, but there is no more confident display of virtuosity. The Sainsbury wing is a rebuke to the defeatism of those who believe that private patronage can never be a substitute for the public sector. As at the Tate, such patronage is available if the conditions are right. The National Gallery extension was a hopeless case in the hands of government, reaching its nadir in the concept of a mixed commercial development. Round the corner in Covent Garden the Royal Opera House was still struggling for permission to build offices and flats that would cross-subsidize its ambitious rebuilding. Similar difficulties afflicted the South Bank centre. Gigantism leads to complexity and complexity leads to postponement and demoralization. Schemes of such magnitude seldom get off the ground.

The Sainsbury and Clore galleries are proof that a revival of confident British architecture – albeit with American help – can be built on a base of private sponsorship. London in the 1980s saw new privately funded ventures not only at its two principal galleries but also for the Courtauld collection at Somerset House and for the Museum of the Moving Image on the South Bank. Getty took on the funding of the National's acquisition programme. London's most impressive display of modern art is by courtesy of the private Saatchi collection in Maida Vale. I cannot believe that there are not more benefactors in the boardrooms and banking houses of London and New York, waiting only for the proper courtship ritual to be performed.

The difference between London and America lies not in the relative availability of money but in the enterprise of potential recipients. Steeped in a public-sector tradition, trustees, directors and custodians have found it tedious to ask individuals to part with their money, easier to resort to the taxpayer. Some have found fundraising ideologically objectionable. Some have found it beneath their dignity. Others have found it beyond their ability. Yet time and again money is found for worthwhile projects, found by those who know how to ask. Wordsworth's message remains as true of the kings of commerce as of government: 'Give all thou canst; high Heaven rejects the lore/ Of nicely-calculated less or more.'

Venturi's building is a monument to this revival. It is a house fit for Van Eyck's *Marriage of the Arnolfini*, a fusion of art and money, of beauty and ostentation, of Europe and America. The Gallery carries forward the Classical humanist tradition with bravura, flourishing its humour, defying Stygian criticism. May it be widely imitated. London architecture has seen too many cold months. Spring is come at last.

4

THANK GOD FOR TOURISTS

ART HISTORIANS have begun to hate people. People clutter up their galleries, ruin their beloved country houses, disregard their opinions and fail to buy their books. Worst of all, people become tourists. And tourists, in the view of art historians, are redesigning Britain after their own image. Their Britain is a monstrous hybrid. It is commercial tat born of entertainment, with history as a distant cousin. Theme Park Britain is its name.

The latest to take up the cudgels is the erudite Joseph Rykwert in the pages of the *Times Literary Supplement*. He sees a blight called the 'continent as museum' spreading across the map of Europe. Mass tourism, he says, is becoming a threat to 'high culture and its conservation'. Outside the cave at Lascaux, itself a facsimile, he notes a metre-high basket filled with spent flash-bulbs. This is outrageous. Outside St Peter's in Rome, he is appalled at the spectacle of Michelangelo's columns festooned with discarded fizzy drinks cans. On entering Hagia Sophia in Istanbul he is accosted by two young visitors asking him the way to Topkapi since 'there's nothing to see in here, is there?' A shudder passes down the professor's fastidious spine.

According to Rykwert mass tourism has broken us from our past and invented something wholly new. Europe has become a museum. Ancient pilgrims, ancestors of present-day tourists, used

34

to visit religious shrines because for them these shrines had spiritual meaning. They might defile them and litter them and even ruin them. But the inherent purpose was one of veneration. 'In substituting museums for religious shrines as pilgrimage centres,' Rykwert writes, 'our society has dissociated hand-made objects and gathered them in museums . . . kettles for looking at are different from kettles for boiling water.' The tourist is no longer searching for a geographical reference point, a physical link between himself and his framework of belief. He has broken the golden thread of history. His quest today is for a stagnant nostalgia that might supply some vague reassurance about the future. Rykwert calls for a new Reformation. He wants to restrain an excessive reverence for the past and the pressures to which it gives rise. He wants to stop tourism.

I find it hard to discern anything coherent in this demand. It is certainly shared by some odd political bedfellows. Some on the New Right find all outbursts of mass culture odious; any intrusion of the multitude into the holy places of history is bad and probably dangerous. Others, on the Old Left, deplore the élitism of preserving old hierarchical emblems. A fixation on the past is unhealthy and reactionary. Caught between such rocks and such hard places, the conservationist is uncomfortable. He wants to harness an undoubted public enthusiasm for historic structures and artefacts to the cause of their preservation. This means he must compromise. He sees no alternative if buildings are to be preserved, and preserved with the public's money.

What is Rykwert really expressing, beyond an irritation at his favourite shrines being crowded when he chooses to visit them? Does he want to withdraw passports from all but the most eminent scholars? Will he suppress travel to historic places? Does he wish to restrict entry to monuments to those who can show some capacity to appreciate them? Does he want to license and restrict any marketing of the European heritage and ban the sale of souvenirs?

What is unhelpful and offensive is the portrayal of the cultural tourist as an idiot drone, gormlessly roaming Europe in pursuit of some facile satisfaction. I too have watched the thousands disgorging from their coaches to gawp at the Sistine Chapel or the National

35

Gallery, and wondered what on earth is passing through their minds. Most look bored and exhausted. But they probably think I look the same. We are all tourists. Education and wealth have led to more intelligent people wanting to travel, and having the means to do so, even if on package tours. They may not derive from Europe's monuments the aesthetic intensity of a Rykwert. But to suggest that cultural tourism is not worthy of the effort, indeed should somehow be stopped, is tendentious. It betrays the ideal of art as an educative process and betrays the work of those who teach it. Tourists may not be scholars. Their working lives and restricted means may require them to travel at peak times – inconvenient for them as it is for the rest of us. They too may find the crowd distasteful. But even two minutes before the *Pietà* is better than none. The tourist who has just three days to spend in Rome is not thereby an illiterate prole.

If blame must rest anywhere for the growth of such tourism, it presumably lies with the writers and teachers who have popularized art history. In English sixth forms, the subject is becoming a favourite A Level course, especially for girls. These courses are the spawning grounds for the youthful hordes crowding the museums of Europe. Rykwert calls them 'parasites' with whom he contrasts their 'élite predecessors' of fond memory, the Grand Tourists, the scholars, the apostles of high seriousness. But why lead so many young horses to the water of learning and then deplore their thirst? Is it that the horses pay good salaries? As a more sympathetic historian, David Lowenthal, has observed (in *The Past is a Foreign Country*), the past is a land in which we all live. It is everywhere. You cannot parcel it up and allocate it to classes or divisions of mankind.

That modern tourism throws up painful choices is beyond dispute. Britain now expects to welcome, if that is not a euphemism, 25 per cent more visitors every five years. As people get richer and win ever more leisure – and despite recessions they still do each year – they find faster planes, bigger airports, smarter hotels, Channel Tunnels, all making the four corners of Europe more accessible. Just 6 per cent of Japanese travel abroad; by the year 2000 the proportion is expected to rise to 50 per cent. Similar figures apply to the United States of America. Yet the resource

they have come to see, old buildings, towns, museums and galleries, is finite. We are building no more Westminster Abbeys. We
seem to have lost the art of creating new monuments of instant
appeal. The Victorian age produced Crystal Palace, Big Ben and
the Eiffel Tower: Europe's closest contemporary equivalents are
Eurodisney and Paris's Pompidou Centre. Equally finite is land for
the roads, hotels, car parks and restaurants demanded by visitors as
part of their 'visiting experience'. There is no Malthusian solution
to this problem of numbers. It is real.

Already Venice and York are shutting their gates in peak
seasons, like medieval cities defending themselves against the
plague. Historic gardens such as Sissinghurst are introducing timed
tickets. Access to some monuments will have to be rationed in the
same way that access to the theatre and music is rationed, by
convenience and price. When Michelangelo's *Pietà* was loaned to
the Metropolitan Museum in New York, a moving pavement had
to be constructed in front of it to keep the crowd moving. 'Dark
tunnel' attractions such as the Jorvik Viking remains in York corral
viewers into cars so that the time they spend appreciating the
exhibits can be controlled. If the queues get too long, the speed
of throughput can be increased. These may seem crass methods
of treating the experience of art, and are easily satirizable by the
Rykwerts of this world. But they are ways of managing popularity.
And popularity is as old as the shrines themselves. Deploring it is
no solution.

No modern assault on historical monuments is, I imagine, as
devastating as were those of past history. The Crusades and pil-
grimages were traumatic to the tribal communities on which they
descended. The routes to Canterbury, Vézelay and Santiago de
Compostela were littered with rubbish, knick-knacks, tricksters
and beautiful churches. The detritus has delighted archaeologists
ever since. The waystations of the Grand Tour were infested with
ostentation, hypocrisy and money, much to the gratification of all
concerned. The tourists raided the sites of antiquity and, in the
view of some, depraved and corrupted the peoples of the Mediterranean. The advent of railways and steamers led to a tourist dias-
pora that appalled the aesthetic sensibility of the Romantics. The
Europe of Thomas Cook, Baedeker and Murray's Guides bred

its own 'anti-tourists' who deplored the 'cockneyfication' of the continent. There is nothing new about tourism and nothing new in the backlash. Yet the result has been the adornment of European civilization, from Chaucer through the Augustans to the Victorian revivalists. It has produced great houses, great collections, great art and the permeation of European culture across the empires of the world.

The boom in replicas, reproductions and prints is deplored by Rykwert and others as yielding nothing but 'tawdry imitations'. What of the eighteenth century's copperplate engravers, itinerant copyists and plaster-cast makers? Were Canova, Pompeo Battoni and the Grand Tour hangers-on all 'parasites'? Are models and casts not better than the depredations of an Elgin in Athens or a Belzoni in Egypt? As for the despised colour photograph, art historians too use them in their books. They are surely an advance on cheap engravings. Certainly it is sad when original artefacts are removed from the places for which they were meant and incarcerated in a museum. I share Rykwert's dismay at such removal where it is unnecessary, and wish we could find a way of returning objects, statues, even buildings, where conservation no longer demands they be held away from the place for which they were designed. Van Eyck's altarpiece, *The Adoration of the Lamb*, has a context in its chapel in Ghent that is gone from Van der Weyden's *Last Judgement* in its air-conditioned room in Beaune. Yet art historians are not prominent in pressing for the restitution of monuments to their countries of origin.

This is a discussion of gains, losses and compromise, not about absolutes. I believe what Rykwert and his friends are demanding is not a Reformation but a Counter-Reformation. They are seeking not debate but relief from debate. They wish to leave the nave of culture and retreat into the chancel, behind a rood of historicism. They may emerge to grant an occasional confession, sell an occasional indulgence. But the holy mysteries must be kept aloof from the masses. The Vulgate of Great Art must not be translated into the vernacular. As Shaw said, all professions end by being a conspiracy against the laity.

I am puzzled at why a public yearning to explore, however inadequately, the meaning of the past should be seen as a sign of degeneration, of spiritual weakness. What is wrong in searching the trace elements of European culture for reassurance? What more reliable protection is there against 'future shock' than the evidence of history? As societies change – in the view of many with ever-increasing ferocity – that change can seem threatening to many people. Why abuse those who seem to find some solace in the relics of history? If they are indulging in ancestor worship, are not we also? An affection for old buildings and the objects they contain seems a commonsensical balance against the shock of the new. It is healthier and less dangerous than a recourse to religious intolerance or political reaction.

Europe is not alone in having a past, or in loving it. The tourist sites of America, Africa and Asia are as popular and as crowded: the Taj Mahal, the Great Wall of China, Luxor, the pueblos of New Mexico. Where Europe is pre-eminent is in the magnitude and richness of its past, the care shown in preserving it, and the ease with which it can be appreciated. In Europe, history is everywhere. Its built environment is a 'past-present continuum' and one of enduring appeal to visitors from other continents. That more visitors want to see Europe each year is not a bad sign but a good one. Those who respect cultural longevity will want to see it preserved, and to pay for that preservation. The historic monuments of Britain, for instance, have benefited hugely from a century of enthusiasm from Anglophile Americans.

A sign of the times has been the growth of the movement in Britain to preserve not just monuments but townscape and landscape. Since the 1960s this has drawn strength not from any cultural élite but from an overwhelmingly sympathetic public opinion. The enemy has chiefly been commerce, politicians and many in the planning and architecture professions, some with a financial interest in demolition and redevelopment. In the 1960s and '70s, architects seemed to agree with one of Hazlitt's more philistine remarks, that 'a constant reference to the best models of art necessarily tends to enervate the mind'. Better to rid the world of such models, demolish old buildings, and start again. The heirs to the 'clearance mentality' of that terrible half-century of 1930–80 are still with us. They take a long time adying. It would be ironic if their place in the destroyers' pantheon were to be taken by art historians.

Venice is a case in point. Time was when its transience, so Ruskin thought, was the essence of its beauty, like that of a girl's face. Jan Morris believed the city's monuments should be permitted 'the slow dignified decline into age and dust which is the privilege of all living things'. I recall gloomy documentaries being made in the 1960s, including one from James Cameron, on the theme that ours would be the last generation to witness the Queen of the Adriatic in her glory. Venice would sink and be gone, a memorial to Gibbon's reflection that man's 'monuments, like himself, are perishable and frail, and in the boundless annals of time his life and labours must equally be measured as a fleeting moment'. The case was hopeless, so let us make a virtue of necessity. Others such as Venice in Peril were made of sterner stuff – and thank goodness. Yet no sooner had the battle to protect the city from the waters of the lagoon been won than we were warned that it faced a fate almost as bad, from tourism. This threat was part physical – the sheer weight of visitors on piazzas and bridges, the pollution of air and water – and part social, driving out residents and stripping the city of its economic diversity. As a result Venice was no longer 'real'. It had become that horror of the museum-loving classes, 'just another museum'.

This is morbid nonsense. Venice was saved with money. The money was forthcoming simply because the world was not prepared to see Venice go. Likewise in 1966, money ensured the restoration of Florence after a flood inundated it with six feet of oily water. I do not doubt that money will save Venice and Florence many times over. Crowds and money are synonymous. Tourism is what sociologists call 'the empowerment of the crowd'. Cultural tourism should direct that power towards sensible conservation. It is surely no surprise that democracies are more conservation-minded than dictatorships. It was Stalin and his successors who destroyed the lanes of the Arbat and tore down the suburbs of old Moscow. It was Mao Zedong who demolished the walls of Peking and created the free-fire zone of Tienanmen Square. It was Ceacescu who wiped the medieval churches of Bucharest off the map and smashed the villages of Transylvania. Democracies may do awful things to the environment but not as dreadful as these.

Historical Europe can no more be made the preserve of a

scholastic bourgeoisie than it can be left to the mercy of dictators or property developers. Europe's ancient monuments are still what they have been throughout their history, places of public resort and symbols of the communities in which they stand. Mark Girouard has shown that medieval castles, even early country houses, were like monasteries and abbeys, open to all, to princes and paupers, knights, travellers and peasants. A big house was a local point of security and shelter, of deference and loyalty, of companionship and culture. Only in the eighteenth and nineteenth centuries did the owners of such buildings retreat behind their walls and make them the exclusive domains of privilege. The crowds now pouring into Stokesay and Berkeley Castles are merely re-enacting the crowds that would have occupied them at the time of their construction. I have wandered through many empty houses, in the Veneto, in Sicily, in Scotland, France and England, often in the company of learned custodians, and found their emptiness depressing. I recall visiting Calke Abbey before its opening to the public. Its jumbled rooms and impedimenta were senseless without people moving among them, even possibly damaging them. Damage can always be repaired. An ancient family house in Long Melford, opened occasionally to the public, invited children to play with the toys in the nursery. The room was alive in a way inconceivable had it been roped off and protected. Stolen toys can be replaced.

Only a few of Europe's masterpieces are truly overrun. We can appreciate in relative peace even the Vatican, Westminster Abbey, the Louvre or St Mark's Square if we accept the inconvenience of travelling off-season. On a bright December morning I have had the Acropolis to myself. Five minutes from a world-famous site I can usually find seclusion and peace in a monument almost as rewarding: St Stephen Walbrook near St Paul's, Santa Maria dei Miracoli near St Mark's, the tapestries of the Cluny near Notre-Dame, the Amalienburg near the Nymphenburg. The Trevi is anyway best after midnight; the Alhambra best in winter. Not for many decades will most of the buildings on the books of the National Trust or English Heritage be bursting at the seams, except at the height of the season. I am sure both organizations will supply lists of treasures which visitors can enjoy alone most months of the year. Elsewhere the unsung, even the undiscovered, delights of Eastern Europe are silently awaiting study, repair, affection and appreciation. There is room and to spare for tourists.

There will always be serious debate between scholars and those in charge of monuments under pressure as to how best to conserve and display them. Architectural maintenance must be married to the management of crowds. Big buildings have wrestled with this problem since they were constructed. The evolution and layout of London's Hampton Court is a vivid illustration of how a working palace found itself constantly short of space and having to tack on extra quarters to meet the demands of occupants, visitors and staff. Thousands of feet tramped its corridors and degenerated its fabric before modern tourists arrived on the scene. Nowadays most damage to fabric is due to traffic in and around popular sites. In future cars and coaches will be drastically curtailed to restrict vibration and atmospheric pollution. At Stonehenge, visitors will be told they must walk half a mile if they want to see the stones at close quarters. Germany's historic buildings, never designed as a backdrop to motor vehicles, are being shielded from cars. They must be approached on foot (or perhaps horseback) or not at all. This is prudence: rationing perhaps, but not exclusion.

Likewise inside historic buildings, pollution is eroding delicate materials, as candle grease and human sweat did of old. In time this means more facsimiles, recreations, wholly new designs. The demand for interpretation will involve more investment in special displays, in tableaux, in dramatic performances. Argument is bound to rage whenever a building is damaged and must be restored or replaced. This was demonstrated recently after the fires at Hampton Court, Uppark and Windsor and at the Hofburg in Vienna. These debates repeated in a minor key the great argument that preceded the majestic rebuilding of old Warsaw after it was burnt and razed in 1944. Should the guardian of the past invariably 'leave as found', or should he accept that the past is merely another form of the present? That the answers to these questions are not self-evident is what makes conservation so stimulating a pursuit. But excluding the public from consideration is surely not on the agenda.

Tourism must be planned. The tourist will want to see a monument or artefact so as to derive historical meaning from the experience. It cannot be a manifest pastiche, decked in the trappings of commerce. It cannot be just a stage set. Dark tunnel displays without authentic relics (for instance in Oxford) have proved less attractive than those with them (as in York). The public has been educated to expect authenticity and cannot be cheated. In the long run good taste will triumph, as the National Trust has shown over years of custodianship of country houses. I am sure that the ugly commercialization of France's Mont St Michel will be to its long-term detriment, compared with its carefully preserved English counterpart, St Michael's Mount in Cornwall.

One scholar offended by tourist pollution does not make a cultural winter. As long as enough people care about the future of the past, the past will be in safe hands. Five million West Europeans now work in tourism. Postwar Europe has shown it can absorb huge numbers of visitors, far more in the 1990s than would have been thought remotely possible in the 1950s. It will absorb ever more. More than any other continent, Europe is rich both in masterpieces and in lesser treasures. Nowhere else manages to feed and clothe all its people, accept constant immigration and yet conserve its past for all the world to enjoy. If Europe is 'just a museum', it is a remarkably vital and successful one. Europeans have perpetrated many horrors against their collective past. But the European tradition is to contest, argue, fight and compromise. This is not a sign of social and moral decay. It is a sign of life.

5

THE COUNTESS OF CHINCHÓN

THE SPANIARDS have conquered at last. They have done so not
at Greenwich, where the Armada show spreads itself across the
Maritime Museum, but in a discreet room at the National Gallery
where a single work of art is on display. It is Goya's portrait of
the Countess of Chinchón, released for a while from its Madrid
captivity. The display is what Coleridge called a 'secret shared with
the public and very well kept'. The Gallery is poor in Spanish art.
One of its former directors, Kenneth Clark, excused his neglect
of Spain in his television series *Civilization* on the grounds that
the peninsula had produced 'so little to enlarge the human mind
and pull mankind a few steps up the hill'. What an extraordinary
prejudice. The Goya normally hangs in the drawing-room of the
Duchess of Sueca in Madrid. Rumour has it that it was lent after
a personal request from the Prince of Wales. If so they both
deserve our thanks.

Writers on art disdain hyperbole in discussing paintings. They
claim that the English adjective can never do justice to the swirl
of a brush or the hatching of an etcher's needle. Perhaps. But how
else to plead with the reader to go and see a work that he or she
is unlikely ever to have seen, or ever to see again? I can only say
that this is one of the loveliest paintings on which my eye has ever
come to rest. I approached it as a sceptic, normally regarding

Goya's rushed, hot-blooded style as brilliant but not in the first division. The coarseness of his portraits made him no match for a Rembrandt or a Hals or even a Reynolds or a Gainsborough. He seemed embedded in eighteenth-century Spain, a land still struggling to emerge from the Middle Ages and constantly on the brink of sliding back. Goya was the nightwatchman of that brink. He prowled it throughout his life, straining towards Géricault and David but dragged constantly back to the world of Hieronymus Bosch. He never resolved the ambiguity and lapsed into deafness and despair. Not my sort of painter, I thought.

How wrong I was. On entering the National Gallery's Room One, I saw in the distance what could almost pass for a Gainsborough. A young lady, perhaps no more than a girl, is seated on a chair, dressed in white and gazing not at the viewer but into the middle distance. At first glance the work seems a society portrait, not worth any particular fuss. But Goya's eyes are always compelling. Fasten on to them for a minute and you feel the whole composition begin to move. The dress starts to shimmer in the light. The torso seems to shift, as if about to stand. The mouth, now with just a hint of a smile, is about to speak. You come suddenly to attention, ready to listen.

Yet the key to this picture is not in the eyes but in the background: a background not of wall or landscape or emblems of Hispanic status but of an utter blackness. The black is thick and rich, advancing and receding as if offering the girl up as sacrifice, then claiming her back. The longer I gaze at it, the more its density seethes with the images that beset this young lady's life, dark images of Spanish history and even darker ones from the melancholy depths of her experience. Here is the bright innocence of enlightenment set about by black Spain. The painting was executed in the spring of 1800, with Madrid enveloped in both political and intellectual turbulence. The historian Gwyn Williams wrote of Goya's work at this time that his 'psychological penetration implies personal, sometimes obsessional, interest . . . These paintings, which approach self-portraits in their tension, are in effect autobiographical.' If such could ever be said of a painting of a young girl by a middle-aged man (Goya was then 54) it could surely be said of this one.

The sitter was Maria Teresa de Bourbon, Countess of Chinchón, cousin to the King of Spain. Her delicate complexion and red hair reflect a part-Scottish ancestry. Goya had first painted her as a child and now portrays her at the age of 20 in a moment of crisis. She is pregnant and rejected, a victim of the brutal politics of the court of Charles IV. Charles's queen, Maria Luisa, had adopted as lover a 26-year-old soldier named Manuel Godoy. By 1800, Godoy had risen in influence to be more than a paramour; he was chief minister and from 1792 effective dictator of Spain, an eminence he held for some fifteen years. He had imprisoned or killed his enemies and forged a wretched alliance with France, whose no less scrupulous leaders treated him with understandable suspicion. Godoy's chambers at the palace at Aranjuez were magnificent, linked by a gallery with those of the Queen, by whom he had fathered a royal princess. Godoy was the epitome of a degenerate and paranoid autocrat.

He was more than a lover, he was a philanderer. Such was the Queen's jealousy that she compelled him to marry her compliant young cousin, the Countess of Chinchón. Godoy went through with the ceremony, made the girl pregnant but immediately dismissed her and returned to the royal palace. It appears to have been at this point, with the Countess sheltering at her parents' house outside Madrid, that Goya was commissioned to paint her portrait. Goya had become a court painter in 1789 but an illness in 1792 left him stone deaf, an event that seemed to give his paintings a new emotional charge. Nor did it prevent him achieving the highest honour of First Court Painter in 1799 at the age of 53. The following year he produced not just *The Countess of Chinchón* but also his best-known group portrait, *The Family of Charles IV*, with Queen Maria Luisa in all her black ugliness.

Godoy veered between liberalism and reaction in his attempt to keep power. Brief periods of intellectual freedom combined with longer ones of political instability. Medieval Spain, represented by the Inquisition, was challenged by the supposed enlightenment of revolutionary France. Goya stood deaf witness to the resulting chaos. In 1799, the year of his appointment at court, he produced his famous satirical prints, *Los Caprichos*, ridiculing Madrid's politicians, bishops and society ladies. The prints were immediately banned, though such was Spain's turmoil that Goya's position at court appears to have been unaffected. Godoy was still in the ascendant, and Goya was commissioned to paint the *de jure* wife of this *de facto* ruler of Spain. Godoy was to last another eight years, not toppled until 1808 when Spain was overwhelmed by Napoleon's Peninsula campaigns. A no less devastating civil war followed. Blackness triumphed.

How far Goya meant this picture to be read metaphorically is immaterial. Metaphor was the language of much of his art but it is for us to choose how we wish to view it. I see Spain's historical crisis portrayed as love defiled by its brutal leader. Here is a frail girl set alone on a dark canvas. Her pregnancy is symbolized by the ears of corn in her bonnet, still green and unripe. The young woman Goya has known since childhood has been impregnated by a reckless and sinister youth, at that moment leading Spain nobody knew where. Hers is already a loveless fertility. Goya's biographer, Antonina Vellentin, sees her 'on the verge of trembling, as if holding back tears of pity for herself'. But I wonder if pity is all that Goya wished to express. Did he also wonder if she might carry in her womb the promise of a new Spain? Might those ears of corn one day ripen and prove the fruit of enlightenment?

Never has a picture so embodied female vulnerability to masculine cruelty. Goya captures, better than any portrayal of rape, the moment of a woman's submission to a power beyond her control. In the diminutive form of Maria Teresa, Countess of Chinchón, white Spain fights black Spain and woman fights man. Goya's brush never lied. All his life he felt the timeless tension between reason and tradition. This tension, says Williams, 'was to stretch the mind and spirit of Goya on a rack almost as fearful as that of the Holy Office [the Inquisition]'. It drove him close to madness. At this moment of transition in Spanish history, Goya produced a crossroads painting. He gathered up the accumulated tragedies of the past, worked them furiously into his canvas and hurled them at the future.

The Countess of Chinchón rarely travels and may never be seen in Britain again. When I complained of the unobtrusiveness of the exhibition, the National Gallery said there was no money to publicize it – no charge is made for admission – while 'union agreements' forbid the picture being on view in the evening or on a bank holiday. The delight is to be had by leisured *cognoscenti*. How Goya would have lampooned all this. How tame he would have thought our submission to so insipid an authority. He would have daubed two *Caprichos* graffiti on the Gallery wall, 'Old London fights New London!' and 'Come smash the doors of privilege!'

(Written in 1988. Goya's Countess of Chinchón *is now on display at Madrid's Prado Gallery.)*

6

THE PRINCE AND
THE ARCHITECT

I HAVE always sympathized with the Emperor in Hans Christian Andersen's tale of the famous clothes. He was no fool. He liked a good suit and was cursed with simpering courtiers and hysterical subjects. He knew the tailors were tricking him. He knew his courtiers were party to the fraud because they were 'either simpletons or unfit for office'. He humoured them only to see how sycophantic they could be. He would walk the streets naked if necessary to prove their weakness. Perhaps he would find the one citizen brave enough to cry, 'The Emperor's got no clothes.' Andersen gave the immortal line to a child.

The story comes back to me whenever I see the Prince of Wales donning himself in more than the finery of his office. He enjoys adulation not power, but few dare point it out. So he challenges the public with ever more outspoken views. An example was his speech on architecture in May 1984. Self-deprecating humour has long been the saving grace of the House of Windsor. In this speech it was perhaps unconsciously on display. Modern British architecture, said the Prince, was bad because it was 'undemocratic', unresponsive to the popular will. Here was a hereditary prince speaking in one of his more magnificent and autocratic palaces, Hampton Court, but he seemed unabashed. 'For far too long some planners and architects have consistently ignored the feelings and wishes of

49

the mass of ordinary people in this country,' he announced. This was hardly revolutionary or even new, except from a member of the royal family.

The Prince was undaunted. 'What are we doing to our capital city?' he cried. 'What have we done to it since the bombing of the last war? Where are those curves and arches that express feeling in design?' Most of his audience had not drawn a curve in their lives and were appalled at the thought of arches. In phrases that came to define ten years of architectural debate, the Prince said that the City of London's proposed Mansion House Square would 'leave St Paul's dwarfed by yet another giant glass stump better suited to downtown Chicago'. The proposed National Gallery extension, also before an enquiry, was 'a monstrous carbuncle on the face of a well-loved friend . . . a vast municipal fire station'. The speech obeyed one iron law of publicity. It was devoid of qualification. It prejudiced two sensitive planning enquiries then under way, in the City of London and in the West End. And it was spectacularly impolite to his hosts, the Royal Institute of British Architects. The Prince even apologized to the RIBA President, Michael Manser, as he sat down afterwards. The new National Gallery architect, Peter Ahrends, said that the remarks about his work were 'offensive and reactionary'. Architecture had not seen such a good row in years.

One of the Prince of Wales's virtues is his readiness to take aim at targets normally considered immune from criticism, including the professions. Soft victims, such as trade unions or financiers, might involve him in partisan controversy. Those who have sought to keep themselves aloof from attack, such as doctors, teachers and architects, are easier for him to assail; he is not seen to be taking sides in a dispute already in the political domain. But the Prince could hardly have hit architects on a more sensitive spot. He was supposed to be launching a Festival of Architecture, designed to improve the profession's image. The festival was presided over by Manser himself, who was proving a militantly anti-conservationist RIBA president. It involved a bizarre series of dances, lecture tours, jazz concerts and childish games such as 'name your favourite building for demolition' (hardly correcting the image of the architect as vandal). 'Modern architecture is here to stay,' announced Manser, the master of the meaningless aphorism.

Manser's election a year earlier had itself been a statement by a dispossessed professional generation. Made to a younger gathering, the Prince's speech would have seemed rather hackneyed, even if stripped of its clichés. This audience was not young. These were middle-aged architects trained before and just after the war. They wanted somebody to defend their legacy, their tower blocks, town clearance schemes and comprehensive redevelopments. They wanted an apologia for Brutalism, somebody to say that it was a worthy movement polluted by politicians, critics and a misguided public. The principles of Le Corbusier, Gropius, Mies van der Rohe – bigness, functionalism, technology, spareness of line and absence of ornament – were good principles at heart. The British, with their incurable love of the picturesque, had not given them a fair viewing. Such professionals had taken employment after the war with local authorities. They had seen their role as part of a social revolution. Theirs was to be the new Jerusalem, created literally on England's green and pleasant land. They felt they had created just that. They were unloved. Many were short of work.

To these architects, Manser was a breath of air. He told them they were misunderstood by an enemy corrupted by 'conservationism'. Conservation, he said, 'is the end of the line culturally . . . It is sick . . . a monumental deceit.' As for the Prince, he was 'utterly mistaken and wrong'. The royal intervention was 'censorship superimposed above the statutory processes of planning, and therefore within a whisper of being undemocratic and hazardous'. This was music to the ears of public-sector architects and to commercial partnerships worried at the rejection of office buildings by conservation-minded planning committees. All had taken comfort in the upturn in development in the mid-1980s and were determined that nothing should stifle it. Michael Heseltine, sympathetic to the historic buildings lobby, had left the Department of the Environment and been replaced by the more compliant Patrick Jenkin. The anti-development Greater London Council was on the way out. The prospect was pleasing. But here was the Prince blowing raspberries in church. What did Manser propose to do about it?

Not much was the answer. The Prince's intervention was hugely popular. Opinion polls showed that 80 per cent of the public was on his side. Politicians dared not attack him. Both the planning enquiries on which he commented went his way – though the Mansion House rejection was reversed on a subsequent application. Nor could the architects easily find others to blame. Although many of the more celebrated outrages committed against the London skyline were in the name of private profit, some of the worst were by the public sector. The housing estates of Walworth and Tottenham, Newham and North Kensington had been designed on the best of socialist principles. The separation of traffic and pedestrians, with the latter consigned to tunnels and footbridges, had been advocated by Sir Colin Buchanan as the town planning of the future. Its relics, London's first-floor podia, blighted the street frontages of new buildings in the City and West End, most gruesomely at the Barbican and South Bank Centre. Ugliest of all were buildings put up by government: the environment department in Marsham Street, the health ministry at Elephant and Castle, Victoria Street blocks for the Board of Trade, the Metropolitan Police and Westminster City Council. A new Charing Cross Hospital towered over the river at Hammersmith. A new Royal Free towered over Hampstead Heath. The Prince was pushing at an open door and nobody rushed to shut it.

Unlike the products of past architectural revolutions, few of the buildings of the 1970s showed much aesthetic sensitivity. All sides accepted that a prime culprit was meanness, the search for the highest plot ratio at the lowest cost. The closest historical parallel would be the dreary late Victorian façades of Northumberland and Shaftesbury Avenues. Even the most ardent enthusiast could hardly plead for their eventual preservation. They appal foreign visitors and depress Britons who travel abroad and see good modern architecture elsewhere. Evidence that many blocks of this period were suffering from degeneration – the oxidizing of steel reinforcing bars and the decay of cement aggregates – was greeted with delight. They would not be standing for ever. A competition was even held for the replacement of the triple-towered Marsham Street building, backdrop to Big Ben from Waterloo Bridge.

In all this, there was one matter on which the Prince was vulnerable. He appeared negative. His critique had struck home, but what should take the place of modern architecture? What should the sensitive developer, the concerned client, the aesthetic politician do? It took the Prince four years to come up with an answer: an hour-long BBC television documentary *A Vision of Britain*, written and presented by himself. This time an editor and a director were at his side and the effect was remarkable. He had lost none of his vehemence. Now it was not just London but Leeds, Cardiff and Birmingham that received a pounding. The Mansion House took another hit, as did the new British Library at St Pancras, the BBC building at White City and the Canary Wharf tower in Docklands. The camera showed Cesar Pelli, the architect of Canary Wharf, chatting amiably with his clients round a model of his tower. An embarrassed Prince stood aside as if witnessing a rape.

This time the Prince was careful to spend at least half his allotted time saying what he liked as well as disliked. He said he approved of the Classical and vernacular revival, of community-based housing, of new structures that fitted alongside old ones, of colour and decoration in hospitals and schools, of 'banks that look like banks'. Named architects were singled out for praise: Michael Hopkins (at Lords), Terry Farrell (at Charing Cross), Jeremy Dixon (plans for the Royal Opera), Quinlan Terry (Richmond riverfront). His own guru was the neo-Classicist Leon Krier, whom the Prince had commissioned to prepare a 'renaissance' village on his land outside Dorchester in Dorset. The programme ended on a metaphysical note. The latest buildings, designed to what the Prince termed a more human scale, could and should convey a sense of spirituality. They should suggest that 'man is not a mechanical object whose sole aim is to produce money'.

To a public figure whose sympathy towards David Owen's Social Democratic party was well-known, the Prince's outpourings were beginning to look like a political programme rather than just a critique. He was taking a risk. The Prince was espousing the new post-Thatcherism, a marriage of public and private sectors, a pursuit of personal fulfilment rather than financial reward, a sensitivity to nature and the environment even at some cost to growth. More specifically, the Prince was demanding for the public a say not just in the framework of planning but in the appearance of buildings. The bogey of all architects is aesthetic control, planners and committees dictating style, rejecting buildings whose look they dislike. The Prince of Wales wanted the public to dare to be subjective in precisely this way; reticence had not delivered the goods. He wanted people to insist on good architecture, even expensive architecture, as in France and Italy. Those countries had saved the appearance of their great conurbations without diminishing their economic magnetism, indeed conservation seemed to enhance it. Paris, Bologna, Geneva, Munich, Amsterdam did not rank among the poorer cities of Europe. Nor for that matter did the mostly conserved City of Westminster.

What was curious was not that the Prince of Wales should say such things but that any contrary view should have held sway for so long. The regulation of settlements is as old as settlements themselves. The first detailed planning consent I know is in the Book of Ezra, precise dimensions for Solomon's temple. Elizabeth I issued one building regulation after another out of 'respect for the Common Good and public profite of the realm'. Anyone who disobeyed the regulations would be 'hanged from the beam of his house, and let his house be made a dunghill'. The desire to beautify cities has been shared by Greeks and Romans, Indian princes and Arab potentates, Mancunian magnates and American tycoons. None would have thought the Prince's remarks at all exceptional.

Yet architects continued to do so. There was a swift backlash from many in the profession and some critics. Factions emerged, camps formed. The Prince provocatively founded an Institute for Architecture, with prominent Classical revivalists on its board. The RIBA found itself trapped in a fast polarizing argument between what could roughly be classified as neo-Modernists and post-Modernists, the latter even claiming the former's mantle as the true modern architects. The argument was the more fierce because contracts were involved. Battle was joined over many redevelopment sites that came on stream in the boom of the late 1980s, largest of which were King's Cross and Paternoster Square. The former, with Sir Norman Foster as master planner, was to become the exclusive preserve of the Modernists. The latter, inspired by Terry Farrell and John Simpson, was unrepentantly post-Modern, with not a glass wall or concrete box in sight.

Sir Richard Rogers, a leading Modernist, launched a strong attack on the Prince in *The Times* in 1989. He accused the Prince of having had him thrown off the shortlist for the important Paternoster Square project by St Paul's. The Prince was secretive and undemocratic, he said, his nostalgia was rose-tinted, his favourite architects were 'besotted with a past that never existed'. The Prince and his followers wanted just a 'pastiche Disneyland'. They answered to nobody. They had failed to realize that the Modern Movement of the twentieth century represented as drastic a break with past styles as was the Italian Renaissance. It was 'a new aesthetic, responsive to the scientific and ethical movement of the times'. Rogers was not defending all postwar architecture and some bull points lurked among his restless clichés. 'The conservationists are right; much that has been built in Britain since the war is quite appalling and the centres of many of our principal cities have been destroyed. But it is quite unjust to make the Modern Movement or any other movement for that matter the scapegoat for this.'

By now terms were becoming confused. But modern architecture, however defined, was at least offering the public a choice. Although he did not name the architects concerned, Rogers criticized buildings to which he took particular exception. One was Venturi's National Gallery extension, another Julian Bicknell's proposed Moscow Embassy residence. The latter was, said Rogers, 'like a stage set for *The Three Musketeers*'. Not for decades, perhaps not since the battle between Pugin and the neo-Classicists, had distinguished architects gone public with such personal attacks on their contemporaries. The Victorian Battle of the Styles was enjoying a spirited revival, a suggestion canvassed by the architectural historian, Joe Mordaunt Crook, in his 1987 book, *The Dilemma of Style*. Taking a sanguine view of the Modernist backlash, Crook suggested that Modernism was merely another phase of cultural history debased by its followers. It would inevitably be supplanted by something fresh. 'Modernism never shook off the old bogey of association,' he wrote. 'Houses were now supposed to look like machines, just as Regency dairies were sometimes supposed to look like cathedrals. Art Nonsense . . . was being replaced by Machine Nonsense.' Rogers's Lloyds building in the City of London, the ultimate Machine Nonsense, was a good illustration of Crook's point.

Whether or not the Prince will prove to be on the side of the angels, only time will tell. Certainly he appears to be on the side of history. There was bound to be a backlash against the anonymous internationalism of the Modern Movement, and it was bound to take the form of a re-examination of traditional English design, of Classical revival, Gothic, even Tudor and medieval vernacular. By the end of the 1980s an almost Edwardian inventiveness filled the gaps in Covent Garden, Fleet Street and the City. A neo-baroque building was going up in King Street, St James's, and a neo-Gothic one in Mincing Lane. Few buildings, whether residential or commercial, were in the bland concrete and glass that had been fashionable ten years earlier. In 1993, the Prince was asked to open the new Vintners Place on Upper Thames Street, described by its architect Jeremy Mackay-Lewis as being a 'Classicism for the future' and partly inspired by the Vatican. A tower block in the East End was even redesigned with a 'Chippendale' roof.

Architecture in the 1990s found new vigour in returning to its cultural rootstock. 'Eclecticism in some form or other is surely here to stay,' wrote Mordaunt Crook. 'We have had to relearn what the nineteenth century painfully discovered: architecture begins where function ends.' They were the same sentiments that the Prince of Wales had expressed at the start of the decade. The Prince went on proselytizing with speeches, seminars, books and his own patronage as Duchy of Cornwall landowner. His had been one of the most remarkable royal interventions of modern times. He did not convince the architects. That would have been expecting too much. He had attacked them and British professions are more hidebound even than royalty. But he had for once turned the tables on them. He had shouted that it was architects who behaved like emperors – and many were stark naked.

7

THE GREAT FIRE
OF WINDSOR

THE FIRE was started by a spotlight touching a curtain pushed up
against it by a picture frame. Nobody was to blame. From such
mundane accidents arise great conflagrations. So do great debates,
and none was greater than that started by the blaze which consumed six Windsor Castle rooms in broad daylight on a Friday
morning in November 1992. The occasion saw a burst of public
support for the Queen, whose special home Windsor had always
been. Her diminutive figure surrounded by firefighters and staff
rescuing furniture and pictures seemed to symbolize an embattled
monarch in the worst year of her reign, her *annus horribilis* as she
was later to call it.

Battle was first joined over whether she should pay any or all
of the cost of repair. That was stifled with a brisk government
promise that the state was ready to pick up the bill, a brisk under-
taking from the Queen to start paying income tax and a later
decision that most of the repair would be paid for by opening
Buckingham Palace to the public. No sooner was that matter out
of the way than swords were drawn in a more prolonged wrangle.
Should the rooms be restored as they were before the fire, or not?
Seven years earlier, in 1986, an equally destructive fire at Hampton
Court had ruined a number of Wren rooms and their Grinling
Gibbons carvings. Then there had been no argument. The

Hampton Court restoration was hailed as a glory of British craftsmanship. The tools and techniques used by Wren and Gibbons
were carefully repeated. Mistakes made in the original hangings,
for instance wood carvings reversed, were corrected. Even the
seashells used by Wren as insulation between floors and ceilings
were collected, washed and put back again. There had been murmurs from the Royal Institute of British Architects that 'it might
be nice' if a modern British architect were asked to design new
rooms – had not Wren himself 'modernized' the old Tudor palace?
Such murmurs received short shrift. Anything other than facsimile
reinstatement of so important a building was unthinkable.

Windsor was approached in a different light. It was, in its architectural outline and plan, medieval. It had passed through a
number of periods and styles, some more distinguished than
others. Unlike Hampton, there had been no architectural symmetry that demanded reinstatement. The famous skyline had not
been damaged. That this profile was not medieval but mostly Sir
Jeffry Wyatville's rebuilding of 1824 was of no account. He had
even lifted the Round Tower by thirty-three feet to make it more
prominent in the landscape. The result is supremely beautiful, one
of the definitive castle settings in Britain. Seen from the Slough
bend of the M4, Windsor seems to float beyond Eton on a cloud
of Thames mist, the fairy-tale creation of a monarch who, even in
his degenerate old age, remained a man of taste and culture.

So far so good. But what to do about Wyatville's lost interiors?
Here in the east corner of the Upper Ward was a vast pile of
charred rubble. The fire had begun in the chapel, which was completely ruined, as were the adjacent Octagon Room, Brunswick
Tower and State Dining Room. Less ruined were the Crimson
and Green Drawing Rooms, the Grand Reception Room and
St George's Hall. Though these last four suffered severe damage,
including the loss of ceilings in all but one, enough remained for
accurate restoration to be possible on the basis of surviving fragments, rather than the old photographs on which the Hampton
Court craftsmen had mostly to rely. All had had their furniture
and most of their pictures removed in the course of rewiring work,
an extraordinary piece of good fortune. The only serious loss was
a large sideboard by Pugin in the State Dining Room.

Much of the initial debate turned on 'just how good' Wyatville's work really was, reflecting the prejudice that still blights certain revivalist styles of the nineteenth century. Although the interiors were mostly Regency in date – which would have secured their respect had they been neo-Classical and by John Nash – their mostly neo-Gothic character rendered them vulnerable to the historically inaccurate charge of being 'Victorian pastiche'. And was not Wyatville a bit flash? Was not neo-Gothic dishonest? Was not Blore, architect of the chapel (altered by Casson in the 1970s), thoroughly mediocre? The Grand Reception Room was decorated in the style of Louis XV, which seemed less than authentic Regency. To many members of the public who had visited St George's Hall as tourists, the discovery that this huge chamber was not medieval at all came as a shock. Journalists who on the night of 20 November rushed to consult Pevsner's Berkshire volume found to their surprise that the Hall was dismissed as merely '185 ft long . . . low-pitched roof is in fact of plaster . . . no-one would call it very festive'.

If a Regency architect could reinterpret historic styles in this way, why should our own age not do the same? The government's initial statement on the restoration added that ministers 'have open minds as to the preferred architectural style'. The cat was among the pigeons. The President of the RIBA, Richard MacCormac, caused an immediate flurry of feathers. 'There is no question of returning to an authentic design for the castle', he was quoted as saying, 'since one doesn't exist . . . A good solution would be to allow contemporary architects to design sensitively around the historical fabric.' The RIBA called for a competition to select an architect for the rebuilding as 'a far more positive assertion of tradition than a slavish recreation of Victorian pastiche'. The abuse of the queen's name was universal.

The architect Piers Gough, whose work embraced both Modernist and Classical revival, agreed. 'Windsor was not such a pure and wonderful thing that it has to be replaced [as facsimile]. It is an accumulated set of buildings and can go on accumulating.' He even indulged in a fantasy worthy of Brighton Pavilion, a design for a new roof to St George's Hall in the form of the ribcage of a vast dragon. 'St George is supposed to have killed the dragon,' he told the Arts Council's Rory Coonan, 'yet the hall burnt down. I see it as the fire-breathing dragon getting back at St George.' A rigorous Modernism came from Richard Burton of ABK. He proposed a vast steel canopy for the Hall. There were even some to propose that the ruined parts of the castle be left as ruins, to add to the picturesque effect. A cartoon by Peter Brooks appeared in *The Times* showing the Windsor courtyard with a Pei pyramid in the centre in the manner of the Louvre.

The debate was both heated and ironic. The Wyatt family had been leaders of the picturesque revival of the early years of the nineteenth century. Their castles, towers, ruins and follies dotted the landscape of Britain in a profusion of romantic outlines. The old Palace of Westminster was clad in a Gothic facing by James Wyatt, uncle of Wyatville. Some Wyatt creations were hardly more substantial than stage sets, the tower at Fonthill collapsing soon after it was built. The style was fiercely controversial. The young Augustus Pugin danced with joy as a huge fire consumed Wyatt's Palace of Westminster. 'It was a glorious sight,' wrote Pugin, 'to see [Wyatt's] composition mullions and cement pinnacles and battlements flying and cracking . . . The old stone walls stood triumphantly amid the scene of ruin while Wyatt's brick walls, framed sashes, slate roofs, fell faster than a pack of cards.' Pugin would have been no less delighted in 1992 to see Wyatville's St George's Hall decoration peeling off in the heat to reveal the medieval and seventeenth-century walls robustly surviving under-neath. At Westminster it was Pugin himself who won the contract to replace the old Palace with something more Christian and more 'honest'.

Pugin versus Wyatt was a true aesthetic contest. The argument at Windsor was different, between 'no style' – the reinstatement of the pre-fire fabric – or 'new style' which might be anything the client might like. As the weeks passed and more people managed to visit the ruin, the feasibility of accurate reinstatement began to gain ground, and with it the possible scope for innovation. The doyen of Regency design, John Morley, declared that not to restore Wyatville's rooms would be 'cultural barbarism'. Colin Amery of the *Financial Times* pointed out that the Grand Recep-tion Room, 'one of the finest neo-rococo interiors in the world', still had enough plasterwork surviving to be completely restorable. Giles Worsley in *Country Life* concluded that the Reception Room, the Green Drawing Room and the kitchen could be accurately restored. He came to the same conclusion about the Crimson Drawing Room and the ceiling of the Hall: enough sections survived of each for a complete reproduction to be possible.

St George's Hall ceiling was more difficult. It had not been made of real wood beams but was a painted plaster pastiche (properly so-called). Should a pastiche be made of a pastiche? The remaining 'semi-private' rooms, including the private chapel and State Dining Room, had completely gone. What should be done about them? Choosing his words with evident care, Worsley took the view that a modern design 'capable of creating rooms in a more traditional mould which respond to the original furniture . . . is quite as much in the spirit of our times as anything in glass and steel'. He had no doubt that Britain possessed architects capable of such sensitivity. *Country Life* magazine launched its own competition for a design.

It was still not clear to what tradition such a response should be made. The task that Wyatville had set himself at Windsor was to make the castle and its setting a masterpiece of English picturesque. As such, his work was all of a piece. He saw it as a unity, creating what Pevsner called 'one of the most spectacular castle ensembles anywhere'. Pevsner added, 'The naïvety with which the early nineteenth century believed in the possibility of making a better medieval castle out of an existing and faulty one may amaze us now. Yet this attitude, which . . . has given us better picturesque landscape than nature could provide, set Windsor off on the greatest period of its social life, the Victorian.' Regency Windsor, said Pevsner, 'is a curious and unmistakable unison of contrived variety with maintained uniformity . . . an un-medieval, Georgian rhythm'.

Such insight is important. Any restoration of the Windsor rooms that does not subscribe to it is likely to destroy, at least inside the building, the essence of what Wyatville set out to achieve: an architectural processionary route. The sequence from grand staircase through state rooms, hall and reception room was meant to offer variations on a historical theme of chivalry and romance. Each room had a contrasting style, classical, baroque, rococo, but primarily Gothic, thus stating the aesthetic union of all style. The modern critic might not enjoy this eclecticism, but it reflected the ideas of a significant group of artists in a particular period of British taste. It should be decried no more than should Wren's insertions at Hampton Court.

That this procession is restorable at Windsor is beyond doubt, indeed it might be extended into the lost semi-private chambers. When the Victorians set about recreating the spirit of Early English Gothic in their churches, they did so as an act of piety to the past. But they showed flair in creating variations on that theme. That is the challenge of Windsor, a variation on a Wyatville theme. This is no mean challenge. In the case of the roof of St George's Hall it demands a wholly original design. The present enthusiasm for English revivalism has fortunately produced a wider choice of designers and craftsmen than would have been the case a decade ago. The scholarship and the skill are available. A brief to update Wyatville can thus be written with greater confidence of it being met. The spirit of Windsor can be restored, its furnishings and furniture replaced, its pictures rehung. The job is every bit as exciting as building the castle afresh.

8

JOHN BETJEMAN'S HEATHROW

'WHAT INEXHAUSTIBLE food for speculation do the streets of London afford!' I sense that the imagination of Charles Dickens was never put to the test of the eastern perimeter road of Heathrow Airport. Yet here are John Betjeman and myself on a warm summer day. He has previously told me that there are five medieval churches within half a mile of the airport fence. Now the challenge to find them is on. The Poet Laureate is surrounded by deafening jets and a desert of hangars, old sparking plug factories and grim petrol stations. 'Rural Middlesex,' he has been murmuring since we left Hammersmith, as if savouring a claret. 'Rural Middlesex . . . that most hardly used of counties . . . that very best of counties.'

The expedition to discover the ancient villages of Heathrow had been hatched some weeks before over an execrable lunch at the Great Eastern Hotel. Betjeman loved eating in unfashionable places, provided only that the wine was good. I discovered that a good wine list is a feature of old-fashioned restaurants: there are too few discerning customers to drink it up. I had grown to love the wines of the Loire, Betjeman's favourite, in the Charing Cross Hotel, the St Ermine's, Rules restaurant and, many times, at the Great Eastern. Betjeman seemed to relax when surrounded by anonymous businessmen, people who might recognize him but would never accost him. They were besuited and conventional. If they had secrets they kept them in safe places. He shared the comfort they took in faded hotels and familiar food under baroque ceilings. Betjeman was delighted when the restaurant at Charing Cross was named after him – though dismayed when they changed the ancient menu.

Betjeman at this time was still a walker. Our journeys had taken me to Metroland, to Southwark, to Southend and round a portion of the North Circular Road. None possessed so little apparent promise as the Lost Villages of Heathrow. Yet Betjeman portrayed them as the ultimate antidote to airport blues. Anybody with an hour to spare and access to a vehicle, he said, should escape the terminals and head for the perimeter fence, like prisoners making a dash from Colditz. Pevsner's *Middlesex* and a free taxi should be an alternative to meal vouchers for delayed flights.

Before the aeroplanes arrived in 1945 the area of Heathrow was thickly populated and had been so since prehistoric times. When the airport was built, a quantity of Neolithic remains was unearthed on the site. These fields on the Middlesex flood plain, bounded by the rivers Crane, Longford and Colne, were marshy but fertile. Villages were prosperous. Heathrow itself, a medieval hamlet, was obliterated by the airport. But the latter's swift expansion after the Second World War imposed a freeze on the land in its vicinity, partly for future acquisition, partly because it was assumed that nobody would live in new houses so near a runway. Farms, manors, churches, fields, lanes all stayed as they were, locked in the past. Trunk roads and motorways cut separate paths, leaving old byways undisturbed. Don a pair of earplugs and you could here find countless relics of old Middlesex, left stranded by the westward flow of London. Or so said Betjeman.

'To the north', he shouts, waving in the direction of a British Airways hangar the size of Westminster Abbey, 'lies the Berkeley property, Cranford House, or used to. We must go there. Then on to Harlington and Harmondsworth, which has a delightful village green, quite untouched. We next take the old Bath Road to Longford' – screeching jets seem to graze his pork-pie hat – 'then we might take in the reservoirs next to the sewage farm. From there we should be able to look across the moor to the crooked spire of

Stanwell Church. And then there's Bedfont and Hounslow and Feltham and . . .'

Cranford is the place to start. To reach it we leave the M4 at the Air Cargo exit, last one before the main Heathrow link road. A turning off the roundabout leads in fifty yards to one of the most dejected small churches in Middlesex. A little hump-backed bridge over the Crane stream brings us to the church of St Dunstan. Beyond was Cranford House, demolished in 1939. Its grounds are now a municipal park but its stables survive, emptily defying the motorway thundering at their back. The old Tudor church tower juts up from some magnificent yews. Betjeman seems able to shut his ears to the noise of the traffic. He wanders in through the wicket gate, up the path and into the church to admire its Renaissance monuments. In the chancel stands a large alabaster memorial of 1611 to Sir Roger Aston: 'What fun those sculptors had as soon as they knew their customers were dead.' Nearby is a tombstone to John Finall Cook, 1771–1856. He left as his epitaph that he was 'the worst-used high constable in England, which office he held for more than half a century'. It is a old Betjeman favourite and he stands for a minute's silence in memory of the poor man.

'Old Middlesex, where are you now?' Betjeman once wrote, 'Where are your merchants' houses with walled gardens, land-scaped parks, lakes and carriage drives and bridges?' Cranford has gone but others survive. From Cranford to Harmondsworth we could take a number of routes. There is the M4 or the A4, or there is Cranford Lane. This last turns off the eastern perimeter through a housing estate and deposits us in deep country. The lane goes through a wood, over another Middlesex hump bridge and across open fields to Harlington. The church of St Peter and St Paul has a twelfth-century nave and Norman porch and is Pevsner's 'best in outer London'. The Norman door surround is decorated with cats' heads whose tongues are wound round a scroll. The monuments are as rich as Cranford's. This was indeed prosperous country.

Sipson Lane is as rural as that from Cranford. Rows of tall Lombardy poplars rise on each side. A tractor plods across a field, as if determined to prove that the future lies in the dip of its plough and not in the raucous novelty a few hundred yards to the south. Suddenly the lane straightens to cross the M4 link road to the airport. Here blinkers are required to avoid the horrors bombarding the eye: the Post House hotel, the M4 roundabout, rows of landing lights littering the meadows and huge radar scanners whirling in the distance. Equally suddenly, the lane bends and the horrors are gone. We pass an old farm and head for the distinctive cupola on Harmondsworth church, peeping above a field of cabbages.

Harmondsworth has three ancient pubs, a thirteenth-century church, a small green which, to Betjeman's dismay, has been municipalized and, as a climax, 'one of the grandest buildings in all England' set against a backdrop of willows and water meadows. The village has three handsome if unobtrusive Georgian houses. St Mary's church is an architectural textbook. The structure is part Norman, part thirteenth century, part Perpendicular. The Tudor tower wears its cupola like a madcap on a medieval clown. I can think of no more restful place in which to sit while awaiting a delayed flight to Corfu. The Five Bells pub is a blissful alternative to the Terminal Two cafeteria.

For Betjeman Harmondsworth means only one thing, the tithe barn in the manor farm immediately behind St Mary's. I have never known him to linger over a building. He visits it, ticks it off in his memory, decides whether he likes or dislikes it, then presses on impatient. Buildings he likes receive a quotation or a reverent, slightly fey gasp of awe. Dislike takes the form of a malevolent toothy grin: 'Oh my God!' he says, or 'Wouldn't X love it?' mentioning some hated architect or critic. But Harmondsworth barn is not to be rushed. 'That was a church, this is a cathedral,' he says, turning from St Mary's.

From Domesday to the present, a barn has been recorded on this site. This one may be in every textbook of medieval architecture, but it is rarely visited. Betjeman makes his way through the thick mud of a farmyard that is still dedicated to its original purpose. As always when trespassing, he is nervous, but his desire to see inside is irresistible, as is his hyperbole: 'The biggest and noblest medieval barn in the whole of England, built I'd say at the end of the fourteenth century.' He rubs its exterior walling as a tailor might rub fine silk. 'Pudding stone, they used to call it in this part of Middlesex. Beautiful.'

Harmondsworth barn may be one of the monuments of England, but it is in no sense open to the public (see postscript). Getting inside means crawling under rotten but locked doors and up through bales of hay stacked against them. Betjeman, who declares his incapacity when it suits him, can also display an astonishing agility. He enters the barn like a gymnast. He burrows up through the hay with delight, gasping and cheering as the interior emerges through the gloom: 'Oh look, oh look!' Vast oak columns rear up from stone bases towards the roof. 'Purlins, trusses, collars, wind-braces, aisle-ties, wall-plates . . .' – the technical terms pour forth with attendant superlatives. That the building is still used as a barn gives him particular pleasure. But when barking farm dogs arrive he is terrified and cannot depart fast enough. He proudly carries the incriminating hay on his clothes for the rest of the day. He gazes down at it in the car and incants, 'Harmondsworth hay, Harmondsworth hay.'

We battle on under the main flight-path to the remains of the village of Longford, once on the Bath Road but bypassed as long ago as 1929. Fragments of its past can still be discovered, a pub here, a manor there, a stream not yet buried in a culvert and permitted a willow or two. Betjeman's self-parody sometimes gets the better of him. 'I do believe that's the Duke of Northumberland's river we have just crossed,' he murmurs. 'And what a well-laid hawthorn hedge.' This is terrible country. But a mile beyond Longford, and also on the old Bath Road, is the village of Colnbrook, straddling the river Coln, half in Middlesex, half in Buckinghamshire.

The village was an important coaching stage, like Uxbridge one of the first out of London, and thus full of inns and stables for changes of horse. For us it sits intact but seemingly deserted, victim first of the railway then of the aeroplane. Colnbrook is a remarkable survival. Its inns are museums of the stagecoach era, the George, the Star and Garter, the timbered Ostrich. Nobody appears to have invested a penny in the place for decades. In one of its cottages was produced in 1857 the Cox's Orange Pippin apple. The breeder, Richard Cox, is buried in Harmondsworth.

Poor Colnbrook may have to await the obsolescence of both cars and airports for its renaissance.

The western perimeter road here skirts old Stanwell Moor, from where we could once have looked east across fields to the now vanished settlement of Heathrow. Turning into the airport's western perimeter road at this point, Betjeman is insistent that we see if a tiny handful of houses with gardens survives in Burrows Lane, an exposed peninsula between a sewage farm and the main Heathrow runway. It is still there. What relic of some past pattern of landholding is this? The residents must endure a constant barrage of noise. We wonder how long Burrows Lane can last before being rolled flat by airport tarmac or unroofed by the landing gear of a jumbo jet.

Southwards lies another haven. Across deserted acres of tarmac and concrete stands the slightly crooked steeple of St Mary's, Stanwell. Did an early biplane hit it? Nothing else has been allowed to rise above the treeline, leaving a scene of East Anglian bleakness. Stanwell was called by Michael Robbins in his history of Middlesex, 'one of the least spoilt villages in the county'. That was in 1953. It is spoilt now. Already the church is besieged by new estates for airport workers, oozing prosperity. But the heart of the village is there. The fourteenth-century church is a fine one, with a splendid Nicholas Stone wall monument to the Knyvett family inside. There are some small Queen Anne houses nearby and the tiny Lord Knyvetts School defies some future road widener to demolish it.

We have now boxed the compass to the south of the airport. It takes a vivid imagination to conjure any charm from this district. Landing beacons festoon cabbage fields. Hideous fences surround 'restricted areas'. Derelict cars are left in muddy fields. Boarded-up cafés back on to potholed lorry parks. Yet Middlesex does not altogether give up. There is still Bedfont, poking its head above the roaring A30/A315 junction. This place was called Bedefunte in Domesday and the transliteration might soon continue to 'be-defunct'. The surviving ensemble is incongruous. Bedfont sits next to the frantic Staines road but its church, large green and old Georgian house bring a touch of humanity to an unlovable landscape. The church is another St Mary's, only spoiled by Victorian cladding and with a strange wooden tower like a pigeon loft. A Norman porch guards access to important and ancient thirteenth-century murals inside.

Betjeman approaches the church nervously. 'It's the only church in Middlesex that I've never been inside because nobody ever seems to have a key,' he wails. 'Once upon a time the yews in the churchyard were part of a great hedge and cut into fantastic topiary peacocks. The Cockneys would come down from London for the day to see them: "Darn ta Bedfont!" Now they've gone, and the Cockneys don't come any more. And I bet it's locked.' Locked it is, and the topiary peacocks are a sorry sight. Such incidents upset Betjeman more than is reasonable, as if the art to which he offers his devotion is purposely humiliating him. I have seen him laud a building to the skies then, when some custodian is rude or access is denied, dismiss it as 'a terrible place'. He was especially averse to vagrant Irishmen. We once walked across London to see South-wark Cathedral, but had to turn back when he spied some Irish harmlessly drinking on a bench in the precinct. Nothing would induce him to walk past them. The approach to a building is for him a processional way to a shrine. He cannot bear his communion to be upset. Bedfont upsets him. It stays unvisited.

From Bedfont there is a lane to the carcass of the hamlet of Hatton. Adjacent is the remains of an ancient manor house called Pates, discovered in the 1960s to date back to 1500. It would be of immense value were it not so vitiated by its surroundings. We are now back on the banks of the Crane and have come full circle. Betjeman shouts above the roar, 'Look, there's the Piccadilly Line at Hounslow West where the air hostesses alight.'

'No,' he says, 'we will not take the M4 back, but the Great West Road. Past the Gillette building by Banister Fletcher and all those traffic lights we used to race in our motorcars to pass before they turned red. On to Heston and Osterley House – we could stop at Osterley – and then Brentford and Chiswick and that tedious church at Hammersmith and Chelsea and tea . . . Oh the delight of it all, the delight of Middlesex.' And delightful it was.

(This expedition took place in 1973. Harmondsworth tithe barn is now open and in the care of English Heritage. Not one of the

churches mentioned appears to be accessible. The southern per-
imeter has changed beyond recognition with the building of Ter-
minal Four. My unflattering references to restaurants are out of
date. I am glad to report that Colnbrook and its inns are well on
the way to revival.)

9

SEIFERT'S TOWERS

I LAST met Richard Seifert during the battle to save the remains of the Rose Theatre in the summer of 1989. The encounter was a surprise. Five years earlier, when he was 75, he had said that he was handing over the management of his practice to his son John. What was he doing at the Rose? But old architects never retire. They only fade away when clients go elsewhere. Seifert's clients do not go elsewhere. The old man was apparently sticking at the job until he dropped.

The Rose affair cannot have been good for his health. It drove him near to apoplexy. But his touch was sure. A small property company, Imry Merchant Securities, had acquired a site at the south end of Southwark Bridge with institutional backing at the height of the 1980s boom. The boom was nearing its peak. Imry Merchant was heavily indebted. Every inch of the ground had to be developed and let as swiftly as possible. It was a typical setting for a performance by 'the Colonel'. Planning permission was duly gained for what was to be the new office district of Southwark Bankside. Building contracts were let. Existing buildings were demolished. As is normal, Museum of London archaeologists were invited to inspect the site and, at the moment in question, had virtually completed their agreed two-month stay. Suddenly, deep in the mud, 'somebody found a bloody theatre' as Seifert later put it.

If there was one thing Seifert loathed, it was disrupting a contractor's timetable. Imry Merchant might be prepared to hold off a while, worried for its public image. Seifert was worried only for his reputation for prompt completion. He had already waved his wand over the Southwark site and gained his planning consent. Anybody who devalued that consent would have to pay for it. (He later persuaded the environment minister, Nicholas Ridley, to part with one million pounds as the cost of delay.) Seifert proved much the toughest negotiator in those hot summer days.

Efficiency was the secret of Seifert's success. Many years earlier I asked a London office developer why so many property companies used the Seifert partnership when its reputation for aggressive dealing sent shudders down many London planning committees. The answer was simple: 'Seifert returns your calls, replies to your letters, delivers on cost and completes on time. That compensates for an awful lot of badmouthing from critics.' More fashionable architects preferred to see themselves as artists, not businessmen, a view encouraged by the architecture schools. Artists apparently do not reply to letters, return calls or worry about time or money. To Seifert a client was a partner in a business venture, in which it suited all parties for money to be made. The partnership was often close. Although the Royal Institute of British Architects forbad its members from acting as developers, it could not stop them buying shares in property companies. Seifert admitted to Oliver Marriott, author of the *The Property Boom*, that his early patron Harry Hyams advised him to 'pick up a few shares' in his company. Few architects had this sort of relationship with a client. To most, the latter was a natural enemy with whom a temporary alliance had to be struck, often so as to cajole him into spending more on a design than had originally been planned. This may explain why so few clients return to a 'non-commercial' architect, however acclaimed, for a second building.

My first encounters with Richard Seifert were colourful. In the London conservation wars of the 1970s, when every neighbourhood seemed under attack from developers, 'the Colonel' would cruise the battlefields in his burgundy Rolls-Royce. As I watched the pounding, there he would be at my elbow, spare and neat behind his thick-rimmed glasses. He would comment on the trajectory of a shell or tut-tut if one of his fortifications was not standing the pressure. One campaign in which I was involved forced him to save the old City Club in Threadneedle Street. He sometimes found the flak too fierce and would retreat into a 'No comment'. But the essence of Seifert's approach was to get firm planning permission before the public knew what was proposed for a site. The key to such permission was confidentiality and a complete absence of 'noise'. Secrecy was of the essence. Journalists were inherently dangerous.

Seifert first set up in practice in 1934 after training under Richardson at the Bartlett School. He was then just 24. This part of his career is obscure, a few shopfronts being mentioned as extant work. He entered the Royal Engineers in the war and returned to the Engineers in 1946 for two years, being granted the honorary title of lieutenant-colonel. The title stuck to him in civilian life though he maintains he never courted it. It was not until he left the army in 1948 that he appears to have secured substantial commissions. The key to his early success was undoubtedly his closeness to the Jewish property community. With the end of wartime building controls, men such as Maxwell Joseph and Harry Hyams moved swiftly to meet a booming demand for office space. Conventional British architects appear to have been either too slow or too snobbish to chase this business. Many were preoccupied with postwar town planning. For whatever reason, Seifert found himself a niche and filled it. He never refused a commission and always sought to deliver on time, on budget and in confidence. An early product of the relationship with Hyams was Woolworth House on Marylebone Road, completed in 1955 in a light-hearted Festival of Britain neo-Georgian.

By the 1960s Seifert had become a Modernist and was producing large office blocks as if on a conveyor belt, almost all let to government departments. These were the blocks that set his stamp on London and set the critics' stamp on him. The earliest and most famous was the building that came to symbolize not just the world of Seifert and Hyams, but the whole postwar property boom, Centre Point tower at the foot of Tottenham Court Road. The tower, completed in 1963, was an early example of 'payment in kind' for planning permission. The developer would offer a benefit to the local council, usually land for a new road layout, in return for being allowed to breach the neighbourhood height and density regulations. It was a dreadful way of financing public projects. The architect or developer could hardly be held to blame for the outcome. The fault lay in the concessions made by politicians and planning officials. In the case of Centre Point the new road layout (which wiped St Giles High Street from the map) was soon abandoned for a one-way roundabout. The public benefit was illusory. The scenic damage was permanent.

Such deals wrecked London's policies on density and skyline. They contrasted starkly with the rigid controls operated by cities such as Paris and Washington. Centre Point tower had twice the bulk normal for this part of the West End. Such deals should have brought intervention from central government, except that in London central government was an even worse culprit. The Macmillan Cabinet overruled the London County Council to permit the Shell Centre and Park Lane Hilton to breach height restrictions. These permits were pure gold to developers. As Seifert said in a letter during the Centre Point negotiations (after he had his planning permission), 'We shall be glad to discuss any amendments. But it is most important that the bulk of the building be not reduced.' Bulk was money. Planners fixed the bulk. All that could reasonably be laid at the architect's door was the quality of the cladding.

Compared to many blocks put up in this period – dreary façades in Victoria Street, Oxford Street, Holborn or Queen Victoria Street – Seifert's buildings at this time were mildly interesting. Centre Point's oval plan, its heavily mullioned windows with zigzag openings and its bold ground-floor pilotis came to symbolize the 'neo-baroque' vigour of the Sixties. The Modernist architect Erno Goldfinger dubbed Centre Point 'London's first pop art skyscraper'. At the retrospective exhibition of Seifert's work staged by the Heinz Gallery in 1984, a number of critics confessed that it was the one Seifert building that they found it hard to dislike. To Paul Barker it was 'square-cut and lacy, more of a barmitzvah card than a wedding cake'. *Building Design* called the X, Y and V piers of the pilotis 'marvels of confusion'. Gavin Stamp ordained that Centre Point had been excessively abused. This was almost, but not quite, a critical accolade.

Yet there was more to Centre Point than style. Within four years of its completion, *Building* magazine wrote that 'like the Beatles and Mary Quant this building expresses the supreme self-confidence of sheer professionalism. It has transcended its original role as a building and taken on a much wider social aspect.' The tower soared about neighbourhoods that became famous in the Sixties, Soho, Fitzrovia, Covent Garden. By remaining empty throughout the period (it was not even partly let until the 1980s) Centre Point was the emblem of the sort of property development, and the sort of architecture, that Londoners loved to hate, 'slide-rule design'. It was obtrusive and useless, profitable only by appreciating each year in Harry Hyams' accounts. The tower was even briefly squatted.

The motifs on display at Centre Point occurred time and again in Seifert buildings, as if cloned by computer from a quantity surveyor's report: Space House in Kingsway (Hyams); Telstar House in Paddington (Hyams); New Court, Carey Street (Hyams); the Press Centre, Shoe Lane; Cavalcade House, London Bridge; the ATV block in Birmingham; Tolworth Tower on the Kingston by-pass. All had the familiar Seifert features of heavy projecting mullions, chunky entrances and a disregard for their surroundings. Entrance doors were uninviting and ground floors were dominated by a clutter of car ramps, loading bays and walls that ignored the sensibility of pedestrians. Such are the swirling down-draughts of Seifert streetscapes that they are rarely free of dirt and litter. Some of his buildings looked smart. His later standard design, a strongly rectilinear box façade of polished granite and glass, can be seen at Euston Square and Store Street. By contrast, the former Odhams site in Long Acre even borders on the picturesque. But most Seifert blocks are devoid of character. Draper's Gardens in the City has a strong horizontal line; the neighbouring NatWest Tower, completed ten years later in 1981 and the City's highest building, has a strong vertical line. It is hard to say more about them than that. The critic Brian Hatton stood in Austin Friars and hurled damnation at the twin monsters, 'Hori' and 'Verti', facing each other across the little street.

The Labour government of 1966–70 baulked at the excesses of the office boom, despite having itself occupied many Seifert buildings. Strict controls on new offices were introduced. But the government was persuaded that the same energy should be redirected at London's undersupply of hotels. George Brown's £1,000 per room hotel subsidy proved the salvation of the property industry, and of its favourite architect. The subsidy was subject to a time limit of completion by March 1973. Speed through the planning machine was thus of the essence. Seifert rose to the challenge. His hotels thundered across West London like a herd of elephants, causing an outrage to which he was impervious. Most were on environmentally sensitive sites, in or overlooking parks and conservation areas. Yet with the moral backing of government subsidy, he could offend such sensitivity with impunity. Once again politics overrode sound planning.

Today the 'Seifert hotels' loom over every vista in Knightsbridge, Kensington and Hyde Park. Their names may change with their owners, and their entrances and interiors may be redesigned, but their outline on the horizon is horribly fixed: the Royal Lancaster at Lancaster Gate; the Park Tower in Knightsbridge; the Royal Garden near Kensington Palace; the Metropole, Edgware Road; the Holiday Inn, George Street; the huge Penta in Cromwell Road. This last is a mere shadow of the 2,000-bed giant Seifert had wanted to erect over Gloucester Road station. There was hardly a hotel built under the George Brown scheme that did not use Seifert's office. Few of these buildings are listed in his *Who's Who* entry.

Reciting lists of Seifert buildings becomes tedious. There are apparently 400 in London alone. As critics mention, Wren's motto of *Si monumentum requiris, circumspice* could be applied equally to Seifert. It is hard to stand anywhere in central London and not see one of his works: the former Times Newspapers building in Gray's Inn Road; the Guiness Mahon Bank in Gracechurch Street; the Sea Containers building at Blackfriars, now with bizarre gold knobs on each corner; the neo-Georgian Britannia Hotel in Grosvenor Square; the Heathrow Hotel; the Metropolitan Police headquarters at Putney; offices next to the Round House in Chalk Farm; renewal schemes for Portsmouth, Glasgow, Bexley, Surrey

Docks; hospitals, railway sidings, bridges. I was once walking along the Regent's Canal toward Camden Lock, an enchanting corner of London in which conservation and private enterprise unite to the profit of both. Across my path lay a heavy pastiche of a pirates' castle built for a local canoe club. The design had been donated by Seifert. There was no escaping the man.

By the time of the Heinz retrospective in 1984 Seifert's office had designed more buildings than had any other private-sector practice, some 500 projects. This undeniably ranked him with the great Victorians in terms of output. It did not bring him popularity. John Betjeman used his name as a synonym for any large and ugly office or hotel block. He would turn a corner and cry, 'Oh no, another Seifert!' irrespective of the architect concerned. Quite why Seifert should have become the butt of so much criticism is hard to say. Partnerships churning out undistinguished commercial blocks, such as Chapman Taylor, Fitzroy Robinson, Sidney Kaye, Elsom Pack, and salaried architects in central and local government, designed more banal buildings than his. Perhaps better things were expected of a man so successful. Perhaps envy was a factor. There was certainly an anti-Seifert reaction among planning committees in the 1980s. A new generation of younger developers, such as Geoffrey Wilson, Stuart Lipton and Trevor Osborne, used architects less associated with the 1970s boom. But Seifert did not mind. There were still loyal clients, still plenty of work.

He was not insensitive to professional or public attack. There were times in conversation when a hint of a whinge crept in. He was understandably bitter at his exclusion from the heights of the RIBA, which showered honours on far worse architects than him. But while Seifert was sensitive, he was not so sensitive as to let it affect his work. In our exchanges over the years, Seifert was always courteous, usually defensive, sometimes prickly, but his references to design were at best cursory. 'I think that's quite a nice building,' he would say, or 'I like it, but you know the critics . . .', or his let-out, 'I think that of its period it's quite good . . .'

Despite an astonishing variety of commissions, the Seifert office never seems to have risked a building of real distinction. A more fastidious practice might have set aside a corner for some talented youngster to work on a prestige project, as a movie mogul might indulge in an occasional art film. Not Seifert. The building factory ground on, employing 300 professional staff at its busiest. He was reported once to have asked the eccentric architect Cedric Price how he had remained so steadfast to one stylistic principle over the years. Price replied, 'It's easy: no work.' If Seifert cried over criticism, he did so in the privacy of the bank.

Is there a Seifert style? The 1984 retrospective – the only time the partnership went on public display – offered a curious ragbag. The show was arranged by the firm itself, not by an architectural historian. As a result, public relations dominated truth to history. John Seifert, Richard's son and successor, was plainly eager to diversify the image of the organization and get away from the images of Seifert past. The result was a plethora of environmentally sensitive and post-Modern designs. There were conservation schemes in Mill Hill, where Seifert senior lives, the Cutlers Gardens renovation in the City, neo-vernacular housing in Limehouse, the much-abused Shaftesbury Avenue fire station in a debased neo-Victorian. There were Docklands wharfsides, hospitals, urban renewal projects in the provinces. Only a small section was devoted to 'middle-period Seifert', to the famous office blocks and hotels. Yet these buildings are the ones which won Seifert the sobriquet of the 'twentieth-century Christopher Wren', and which continue to dominate mention of his name. Nor, as the Rose incident showed, was there any let-up in the commercial thrust of the practice, or in the Colonel's presence in a crisis.

Whether much of Seifert's work will stand the test of time is doubtful. His precast concrete sections and massive steel frames cannot last for ever. These are not materials that are easily restorable, like wood, brick and stone. As the buildings erected during the 1960s and '70s come up for replacement – or preservation – 'Seifert's London' is unlikely to win much affection. Yet the qualification for preservation is not just architectural merit. It is also historic significance. Seifert's period of most spectacular activity, from 1960 to 1980, may have coincided with one of the least distinguished in the history of London architecture, especially the offices and hotels that were his speciality. This was a true dark age. But even dark ages need their memorials. No architect characterized the period as vividly as Richard Seifert. His Centre

Point tower, still looming part empty over the streets of Soho, was instantly recognized as a symbol of its age. Let it stay. This building at least deserves the accolade of preservation.

10

SI MONUMENTUM PEVSNERIANUM . . .

ALL TRUE enthusiasts for English architecture nurse the same dream, to visit every historic building in the land before they die. I dream it while motoring past country churches on soft summer days. I dream it on fleeting visits to provincial towns. Sometimes I dream it as a nightmare: another house missed, another journey wasted, will the ambition never be achieved? But worst of all is the knowledge that there was one man who did it, who conquered this Everest alone. Nobody would ever cap his triumph.

I last met Sir Nikolaus Pevsner in 1975 (he died in 1983) at the launch of a guidebook to an unexciting corner of London, West Hampstead. In an early *Buildings of England* volume he had been uncharacteristically dismissive of the area: 'The houses and streets require no notice,' he simply wrote. He was asked to say a few words to the gathering. I remember being rather disappointed. I had hoped he would stand up straight and tell them in a crisp Teutonic accent that they were all wasting their time. He had visited every inch of West Hampstead and still 'the houses and streets require no notice'. They should all get back to their work. But no, it was a gracious performance before disciples. These were local historians schooled by his example to be exhaustive, rigorous, factual; but schooled also not to be afraid of judgement and taste, even at the risk of seeming a prisoner of one's own time. This was the Pevsner lesson I most valued and which is at odds with much of today's antiseptic art history teaching.

Nikolaus Pevsner's collation of the forty-seven volumes of the *Buildings of England* is one of the pinnacles of British intellectual history. It is not simply a gazetteer, but the application of an educated eye to the whole of man-made England. The eye is fresh and foreign. It knows to separate the wheat from the chaff and is capable of intense affection. In Herefordshire, 'there is not a mile that is unrewarding or painful'. In Northumberland it is 'rough the winds, rough the moors, rough the miners, rough the castles'. Gentle Hertfordshire is 'uneventful but lovable'. Pevsner's epithets will linger round the places he describes for eternity. Nobody who loves English buildings can ever love them alone (except those that Pevsner missed). Enter any cathedral or great house, walk through any village street or Victorian courtyard and Pevsner is at one's elbow, tall, omniscient, an all-knowing German governess. Here is some chamfering you may have missed. Over there is some wayward Mannerism. Could this be a trace of clunch? That plasterer, was he apprenticed to Smith of Warwick? The torrent of facts is unrelenting.

Pevsner was born in 1902 in Leipzig, fleeing the Nazis to Britain in 1934. Like many academic migrants he fell in love with his adopted country and its language, and became addicted to both. Though briefly interned as an enemy alien, he helped to run the *Architectural Review* during the war. He went on to become Slade Professor of Art at both Cambridge and Oxford and enjoyed a long association with Birkbeck College, London. He was a ceaseless author, catholic in his application. His output embraced a standard work on English Modernism, the huge *Pelican History of Art* and an introduction to European architecture. That said, Pevsner sometimes seemed to his contemporaries a man dispossessed. He was a generalist rather than a specialist, a historian of ideas rather than a documentary scholar. He was fiercely loyal to his students and cantankerous with his critics. His forthcoming biography (by Meirion and Susie Harries) draws on his personal diaries and shows him harking back with dissatisfaction to his promising early career in Leipzig. By comparison he saw his postwar writing as the work of a popularizer and communicator.

Yet what a communicator. His monument is the series of architectural guides which he persuaded Allen Lane of Penguin to support shortly after the war. He received no royalties on them, being paid as a salaried employee of Penguin. The first volumes appeared in 1951 on Cornwall and Nottinghamshire and the series ended with his editing of the Staffordshire volume in 1974. Revisions and volumes on Scotland, Wales and Ireland have continued to appear ever since. The work was dedicated to his dictum that architectural history should 'describe and convert'. The dictum was honoured to the letter. The *Buildings of England* is the nearest we have to a Domesday survey of British architecture, at least until the government's 'listed building' green books are computerized. But the green books do not convey what Pevsner conveys. He was too much the humanist for so dry and mechanical a task as drawing up lists. He viewed England (distinct in his view from the rest of the United Kingdom) as blessed with a tradition independent of Continental imports, even as it borrowed from those imports. 'The Englishness of English Art' was the title of his 1955 Reith Lectures.

This English tradition began, as does all building, with the earth. It began with the granite, slate, sand and chalk which Englishmen have dug, quarried, chipped and carted since the start of time. It began with landscape, as does each Pevsner volume (with much help from Alec Clifton-Taylor). The picture sections tend to open with rather unatmospheric photographs of hills and fields to make the point. The Pevsner story then makes its familiar progress, through Norman and Early English, growing grander as it passes Tudor and Jacobean to reach fulfilment in the glories of Georgian and Victorian. Millions of readers must have these categories indelibly stamped on their imagination. No matter how confusing the style of a cathedral, royal palace or town high street, Pevsner appears to keep his nerve. He pores over the jigsaw puzzle, separates the pieces, then worries them into their proper place. It is an astonishing performance.

Pevsner's technique was of meticulous teamwork. He was an editor and chief-of-staff rather than solitary wanderer. He began each volume by ordering detailed research from assistants – many of them German *émigré* ladies – through county libraries and the Victoria County Histories. Mountains of notes would be assembled. These were then passed on to the drivers who planned the itineraries: for thirteen years the 'keeper of the sandwiches', his wife Lola who died in 1963, and later a succession of assistants. Everything was done by car. Each night Pevsner would write up the day's notes while the driver planned the detailed route for the morrow. Apart from the first volume, *Cornwall*, he did not drive himself. Helping Pevsner was a coveted honour but not one lightly or long endured. Turnover of drivers was considerable.

Disaster on a Pevsner circuit was, not to be refused entry by an owner, but to be admitted and forced to accept hospitality. This would wreck a schedule of military precision. Assistants would be either amused or infuriated by the fast pace and rigid framework within which each building was described. There were many errors. I once calculated that there are over fifty facts per Pevsner page. It was certain that mistakes would creep in, as indeed they did. I once lived in a 'Pevsner' building: of his six facts, three were wrong. Mistakes caused him great pain and demanded complicated footnotes in succeeding editions. They were the consequence, he was aware, of haste and delegation. But without both the task would never have been completed. Many criticized the *Buildings of England* methodology, mostly for being insufficiently historical and factually sloppy. But none tried to do better.

Towards the end even Pevsner began to tire. In the later volumes he was helped and progressively supplanted by assistants, some happy collaborators, some distinguished historians in their own right. Ian Nairn gave a Pevsnerian fillip to Surrey and Sussex. John Harris was a combative co-author of Lincolnshire. Two of the most important counties, Kent and Gloucestershire, were left to John Newman and David Verey respectively, Pevsner merely editing the text and visiting some of the places mentioned by way of checking. Of Newman's work he wrote in a typically terse introduction, 'Mr Newman's two volumes on Kent are in my opinion the best of the whole series.' The huge task of updating Pevsner's London books, in the hands of Bridget Cherry, is nearing completion, with its grim subplot of buildings 'demolished since first edition'. All were written in the style of the master, though none, except perhaps Nairn, had Pevsner's zest for the snap judgement.

Pevsner's favourite period was Early English ecclesiastical. But his prime achievement at this juncture in art history was to bring to life the most brilliant and productive period of British architecture, that of the Victorian age. This age is now accorded its due; it is hard to recall the contempt visited on Victorian buildings in the middle third of this century, when widespread urban redevelopment was taking place. Some of the most splendid industrial cities in Europe were those of provincial England, Birmingham, Manchester, Bristol, Liverpool, Newcastle. It was not German bombs that tore out their hearts. Local government did that, seeing Victorian buildings not as polychrome palaces but as black memorials to a Dickensian past. To local Labour parties, they symbolized an industrial system against which they had fought and won. To Conservatives they seemed merely ugly, their demolition a sign of progress. Pevsner's volumes came too late to convert either group in time. Those who wanted to preserve Victorian buildings were simply cranks. The gap-toothed streets of Northern England are the result.

True to his German upbringing, Pevsner was an enthusiast for the interwar Modern Movement. In 1936 he had written dismissively of contemporary British architecture: 'The levelling tendency of the coming mass movement – and a true architectural style is a mass movement – was too much against the grain of the English character. A similar antipathy prevented the ruthless scrapping of traditions which was essential to the achievement of a style fitting our century' (in *Pioneers of Modern Design*). By the 1950s, this radicalism had mellowed and he revised some of his more strident early judgements. But as *The Times* said in its obituary, 'He persistently refused to be shocked at the progress of events . . . deeply founded in the history of the past, he was able to follow contemporary developments with equanimity.' His eye was alert to every sign of innovation, a steel frame, a concrete apartment block, a Cubist house. Committed in most of his writing to the backward glance of history, he felt he must draw attention to its onward march. An 'uncompromising' 1930s Hampstead terrace, he wrote, 'goes infinitely better with the Georgian past . . . than anything Victorian'.

As a result Pevsner perhaps neglected some architects against whom Modernism was so drastic a revolt, in particular the

Mary Davies, wife of Sir Thomas Grosvenor

The Countess of Chinchón by Goya

The Guitar Player by Vermeer

The caryatid from the Erechtheum, in the British Museum

twentieth-century revivalists. He disliked neo-Georgian and Art
Deco. He castigated Wallis Gilbert's Hoover factory as 'perhaps
the most offensive of . . . modernistic atrocities'. Yet such damnation was rare. In a calling plagued by faction, that of architectural criticism, Pevsner was a model of catholicity and even
struggled to appreciate architects such as Blomfield and Lutyens
to whom he was unsympathetic. In the *Buildings of England* he
set aside prejudice to record what he saw, however much he was
prepared to dislike it in print. The outcome could be a catastrophe:
a dismissive reference to Bloomsbury's Woburn Square was crucial
at the public enquiry that led to its demolition. The slighting of
the Victorian town hall at Wigan was likewise used by the council
to justify an application to demolish. But every building had its
mention. Be it a derelict mill in Oldham or a music hall in South
London, if Pevsner's team could find for it an architect and a date
it would be on the page. This generosity in one so opinionated
was a remarkable critical feat.

Perhaps immigrants have a deeper feel for the *genius loci* of a
country than do its natives. As with Wyngaerde, Hollar and Knyff,
the English seem to need others to reveal to them the delights of
their surroundings. English writers can wax learned on the treasures of Tuscany and Provence. We laud the virtues of Venice and
Delhi and Los Angeles. But it took a foreigner (or an eccentric
such as Betjeman) to disclose the stylistic grain of Stow-on-the-
Wold or a chancel by Butterfield or Street. Pevsner did not just
appreciate England, he adored it. To him no adjective was more
potent than 'lovable'. Although his literary style was necessarily
brisk, even staccato, and he was a poor lecturer, his pen could
not resist rambling across the soft contours of Worcestershire or
dwelling on the Italianate citadels of Manchester or Leeds. And
where the architecture was not first-rate, he found richness in landscape and townscape. The opening phrase of the first volume set
the tone of all that was to come: 'Cornwall possesses little of the
highest aesthetic quality, though much that is lovable, much that
is moving. Nearly always, in analysing one's emotions, one will
find that what is remembered is more the setting of architecture
than architecture itself.' All the Pevsnerian resonances are there,
rigorous judgement, emotion, an awareness of the wood as well

as the trees, a sense of the lie of the land. He would weep at the uncontrolled caravan blight on Cornwall today.

Pevsner teaches us that to appreciate English architecture we must comprehend the diversity of provincial England. His books may prove to be a last memorial to the shire counties, to counties not just as political units but as regions with distinctive identities. There was nothing artificial about these identities. The counties of England became counties by virtue of their physical and social geography. This geography was reflected in their architecture as well as in their structure of government. In his introductions, Pevsner was adept at distinguishing county from county, division from division, soke from soke, hundred from hundred, piecing together a nation's culture from the raw material of its architecture. He plunged with equal fervour into Middlesex and Cumberland, Lancashire and Dorset. He brushed aside snobbery and fashion. He disregarded passing items of popular or family history. His reticence in this last respect could be infuriating: the parallel Shell county guides are a necessary companion to a Pevsner. But to him the history of England lay in her buildings and her buildings alone. To know them is to learn a different island story from that of Macaulay or Trevelyan, a more intimate and more vivid one.

The finest epitaph on any critic is that he made us see. Pevsner's eye, peering, quizzical behind his glasses, did more than make us see. It achieved his declared aim of converting as well as describing. It made us angry. He did not do this with any strident call to arms. He abhorred the junk prose which passed for architectural journalism. Like his contemporary Sir John Summerson – relaxed, sardonic, his opposite in every other respect – Pevsner was immaculate in his use of language. He came to English prose as he came to English buildings, eager but humble. A sentence should never be abused, words should never be squandered. He told simply what he saw and felt. From there on the reader was judge.

What we see through Pevsner is an English landscape of peculiar charm, a mosaic of tens of thousands of individually described buildings. His England was of a piece and vulnerable. His work encouraged others in the conservation movement to make it less vulnerable. He was a stern teacher, but few teachers can have seen their lessons so widely read and learnt. Few have left a memorial so beyond emulation.

11

THE FINEST WALK
IN LONDON

LONDON IS not a city of villages, it is a city of walks. Every citizen has his favourites and they are usually close to home. Not so mine. My home may be the gentle slopes north of the Regent's Canal. There are fine walks on those slopes, as on the heights of Greenwich and Harrow and round Hampton. But none can compare with the twelve miles that I am about to describe. This is simply the best walk in London.

The route can be traced on a map as follows: start at Kew Green and enter Kew Gardens, leaving by the Lion Gate; cross the Lower Richmond and Sheen Roads to King's Ride Gate into Richmond Park; cross the park to Ham Gate and descend past Ham Common to Ham House on the Thames. From here the walk follows the towpath, with some detours, downstream past Petersham, Richmond, Syon and back to Kew. The best time of year is early spring. It is not too hot and blossom and daffodils are on parade. The lack of leaf cover also gives this walk its special delight: glimpses of great houses temporarily stripped of their secrecy. But whatever the season, remember that the Thames is always best in sunlight. If possible, wait for the sun.

The road across Kew Green is a terrible scar. Its traffic is never still except when congealed at rush hour. But those who seek a more civilized environment have it close at hand. I always enter

Kew Gardens as a bumpkin. All is well out on the Green. Kew Church and its quaint memorials hold no mysteries. Here the humble courtiers of Hanoverian princes found their rest in what must then have been a riverside idyll. The ivy-hung walls of their Georgian houses on the Green are old familiars. But as soon as I pay my money and pass through Kew gates, I am in the sanctuary of alien gods and their acolytes. I lower my voice. I tiptoe for fear of damaging so much as a blade of rare grass. Here are the spirits of *Pseudotsuga menziesii*, of the noble *Sequoiadendron giganteum*. Through the precincts walk scholarly spinsters like nuns in a convent, heads together muttering Latin. Kew is a place of study as much as pleasure. Its high seriousness must be respected by even the most casual visitor.

Kew is a complete calendar of England's seasons. Though its winter has its moments, notably in the new hothouses, there is nowhere better to observe a London spring. Then the camellias and magnolias are stretching their petals, blossom is foaming on the trees and a carpet of daffodils is spread underfoot. Every Londoner pays his respects to Kew at this time of year. It makes our northern winter worth enduring and renders uninhabitable any region that has no spring. But this is not a visit to Kew, it is a walk through Kew. We pass only the orchids and succulents, the Palm House, the Temperate House and the Pagoda. (Though such is the temptation of Kew that I have often started on this walk, been diverted at this point and gone no farther.) From the Lion Gate along Manor Road to King's Ride Gate is half a mile of pleasant suburb. The hiatus is enlivened by one of London's few, perhaps only, railway level crossings.

King's Ride Gate next to Barnes Cemetery is unobtrusive, indeed hard to find, but it has the advantage of not being a road entrance. It guides us into Richmond almost without our noticing. Some guides like to pretend that Richmond Park is medieval, if not 'primeval', parkland. It is not. The precious expanse has been tended and altered over the centuries. But its Rangers have managed to give it a timelessness, as if of pre-enclosure England, a landscape across which herds of deer drift like clouds on a sunlit meadow and a man could ride for miles without meeting a fence. The 2,000 acres were first designated as royal hunting ground by

Charles I. The citizens of London seized it during the Common-wealth but returned it to the Crown at the Restoration. In the eighteenth century Sir Robert Walpole had one of his sons (not Horace) made Ranger and drained Richmond to improve it for beagling. But it was the next Ranger, Princess Amelia, who pre-cipitated the most famous event in the park's history, by deciding to ban the public any access to it. This led in 1758 to a celebrated court case in which the people of Richmond defeated the Crown and asserted a common law right of access. Ladderstiles were erected round the perimeter. These were followed by yet more litigation forcing the Rangers to redesign the ladders so that chil-dren and old people could ascend them.

The terrain of Richmond is rough and often marshy. Deer have roamed it at least since the Middle Ages and are now conserved at 200 reds and 40 fallows, the annual cull supplying venison for royal and ministerial dinner tables. As a result, every tree and copse has to be surrounded by a neat fence, depriving Richmond of some of the sylvan mystery of Hampstead or Epping. The park is dotted with handsome mansions, many beginning life as hunting lodges and named accordingly. In the middle is White Lodge, now the Royal Ballet School and once the home of the Duke and Duch-ess of Teck. Their daughter became Queen Mary and gave birth in this house to the future Edward VIII. Its upper windows look out towards the towers of the old London County Council's Alton estate in Roehampton, famous at the time of their construction in the 1950s as the application of Corbusian collectivist principles to a rural English landscape. They won a host of architectural awards and are ugly and obtrusive. A party of Russians was proudly taken to see them by the LCC but was more interested in the detached suburban houses opposite. There were plenty of Altons back in Moscow.

Striding up towards the summit of Richmond on a clear day, I find the temptation to keep turning back irresistible. The view towards London from the top is exquisite, offering a more vivid sense of leaving town than any modern Dick Whittington could gain on Highgate Hill. Small wonder so many monarchs loved to hunt here, with their Thamesside palaces secure behind them and the troublesome City well in view. For the moment at least, the sight line to St Paul's is protected from encroachment by high buildings, one of the few strategic policies for London planning that is still enforced.

Each of Richmond's entrances has its own character. Robin Hood and Richmond Hill Gates are swirling pools of traffic. Roehampton and East Sheen lead out from the surrounding houses as if marking the end of civilization at Tolkein's Edge of the Wild. My favourite is Ham, still as it would have been a century ago, a scramble of birch, bracken and scrub, dotted with deer and horses and with falling streams and a lake adding to the picturesque scene. The descent from the summit to Ham Gate is bosky and the lane to Ham Village through the woods past Ormeley Lodge is deep country. Ham Common is a triangular green of rare charm, an expanse of grass decorously set about with mostly Georgian houses. Such a harmonious effect would be beyond the powers of any modern design studio: a sequence of redbrick and stucco buildings, garden walls, gates, trees, flowers, grass, all fallen perfectly into place. What an art we have somehow lost.

Half hidden round the corner of a convent and easily missed is the gate leading to Ham House. The path is marked by an incipient lime avenue with the old house visible in the distance. Polo is played on the right, a modern council school is on the left, a politically correct arrangement.

I find Ham House the most rewarding of all London's palaces. It sits alone as it has always done, behind a row of trees on the banks of the Thames. There is no modern clutter near it. The original rooms, corridors and cabinets are intact and are still animated by the ghosts of those who created them. These ghosts are vivid. Chief among them was Elizabeth Murray, daughter of William Murray, who held the post of whipping boy to Charles I. He recovered from his lashes to win both an earldom and the estate of Ham. His daughter and heiress was blessed with the customary features of Stuart beauty, a strong nose, sharp, wilful eyes and a fierce personality. She married a Suffolk baronet, Sir Lionel Tollemache, who looks from his portrait to have been a kindly man, too kind by far for his wife. She became enamoured of the rising star of the Royalist cause, the Earl of Lauderdale. After his capture in the Civil War, she interceded with Cromwell personally on his behalf and later claimed to have been Cromwell's lover.

Elizabeth and Lauderdale married three years after Tollemache's death in 1669, when Lauderdale, now a duke, was at the height of his political influence. He was the final L of the notorious Cabal ministry. The contemporary historian Bishop Burnet described him as 'large, his hair red, his tongue too big for his mouth and his whole manner rough and boisterous and very unfit for a Court'. As for his wife, then in her early forties, Burnet admitted to once admiring her but now described her as 'a woman of great beauty but far greater parts; had a wonderful quickness of apprehension and an amazing vivacity in conversation; had studied not only divinity and history, but mathematics and philosophy; but what ruined these accomplishments, she was restless in her ambition, profuse in her expense and of a most ravenous covetousness . . . a violent friend and a much more violent enemy'. She might plead in mitigation that she had to survive one of the most dangerous eras of British history.

I find it hard to imagine this unpleasant couple occupying so calm a mansion. Yet they were not here for long. What has preserved Ham is that the Lauderdales fell from grace in 1682 and neither they nor their Tollemache successors had the inclination or the money drastically to alter it. Murray's Jacobean H-plan was changed by the Lauderdales, but only by infilling the recess of the H overlooking the garden and by realigning the old hall. Apart from the eighteenth-century removal of the hall ceiling, the house given by the Tollemaches to the National Trust in 1948 is the house as Elizabeth Lauderdale left it.

So rare are interiors of this period that those at Ham seem more Dutch than English. Everywhere are black and white marble floors, 'barley-sugar' cane chairs, black lacquer tables and blue and white china. The joy of these rooms is their intimacy. Sun streams through doors and down corridors, picking out mouldings, fireplaces and ceramics as if preparing a studio for Vermeer or de Hooch. Ham upstairs is a palace in miniature. Its compact plan contrives to include suites of rooms for both the Duke and the Duchess, the first country house library in England, a chapel, one of the earliest picture galleries (or 'cabinets'), a Long Gallery filled with Lelys, Van Dycks and 'studios' thereof, and a formal sequence of state rooms built to receive Catherine of Braganza. The Queen's Closet is a jewel of a chamber with a view out to the garden, now being restored to its seventeenth-century formalism. Among the pictures is a lovely Reynolds of Horace Walpole's niece, Charlotte. She had to endure marriage to the disagreeable 5th Count of Dysart. Obliged by her sister to explain this betrothal, Charlotte wrote, 'If I was but nineteen, I would refuse point blank. But I am two and twenty and am likely to be large and go off soon.' Her 'going off', coupled with her husband's meanness, saved the house from eighteenth-century alteration.

In front of Ham once stood a row of elms stretching forward to the river, noisy with crows. These marvellous trees were black and gaunt and seemed to imprison the house and its occupants. They are now gone. The Thames at this point is all activity. Eel Pie Island, haunt of hippies in the 1960s, is to the left towards Twicken-ham. The old ferry is still in use, to be hailed from the Middlesex bank with a strong shout of 'Oars!' Those prepared for a brief detour are put down in front of Marble Hill House a little down-stream of Ham. This was designed in 1724 by members of Lord Burlington's Palladian circle for Henrietta Howard, the mistress of the future George II. She was an enigmatic lady. Walpole con-sidered her 'sensible, artful, agreeable but had neither sense nor art enough to make the king think her more agreeable than his wife'. Nobody has decided whether Henrietta had a physical relationship with George, but she would chat to him each night for hours and was popular alike with male and female courtiers. She secured an earldom and pension for her separated husband (whom she had 'married for love and hated for the rest of their lives'). Her own prize was this house. Was conversation ever better rewarded? There must be something in the air of Marble Hill. A subsequent resident was Mrs Fitzherbert and it was here that she met another Prince of Wales, the future Prince Regent, becoming his mistress and later his unacknowledged wife.

The house is worth the detour for one room alone, the Italianate salon on the first floor, which seems to fill the entire interior. The room was modelled on Webb's double-cube room at Wilton, the country house of Burlington's friend, Henry Herbert, who was partly responsible for the design. Marble Hill was merely one of the dozen or so mansions that in the eighteenth century made the Thames valley a linear museum of English architecture. A glide upstream on the tide from central London took one past Hurlingham, Fulham, Chiswick, Kew, Syon, Asgill, Marble Hill, Ham, Orleans, York House and Strawberry Hill, culminating in Tijou's great ironwork gates to Hampton Court. Each house was set in its own grounds. Visitors travelling in ornate barges would have seen lawns, landing stages, pavilions, gazebos and grottoes. This was an Augustan paradise, an English Veneto, the home of Alexander Pope and Horace Walpole: 'Twit'nam, the Muses fav'rite seat/ Twit'nam, the Graces' lov'd retreat.'

More remarkable still, all these houses survive in whole or part. A narrow focus is needed to see them in anything like their original setting, but there are plans to restore the Twickenham riverbank to as near as possible its eighteenth-century appearance. English picturesque is back in fashion. The hardest task will be to restore non-motorized traffic on the river, to re-create Walter Scott's image of the Thames as the 'mighty monarch of the scene . . . who bore on his bosom an hundred barques and skiffs whose white sails and gaily fluttering pennons give life to the whole'.

Leaving Ham and moving downstream we reach Petersham, sheltered behind trees to the right of the towpath. Petersham was always an offspring of Richmond, but an offspring that grew up pretty and married well. Like many Thamesside villages, it was the Commonwealth and Restoration which elevated it from medieval hamlet to fashionable resort. At least five substantial houses in addition to Ham were erected in its vicinity. During the Lauderdale ascendancy, it was said that 'all England was ruled from Petersham'. Since then the village has retreated into itself, fighting off the housing estates that invaded the purlieus of Ham and gritting its teeth against a torrent of traffic. It still has its riverside farm and one of the loveliest small churches in London. The box pews and galleries of St Peter's are among the few in Britain to survive nineteenth-century improvement. Inside lies George Vancouver, who charted the west coast of Canada for Captain Cook and who retired to Petersham to write his journal. The city that bears his name paid for the church's restoration and holds an annual service here in his honour.

Ahead lies Richmond at the foot of its famous hill. A long Georgian terrace rises like a battlement towards the summit where stands the enormous Star and Garter veterans' home. The view upstream from this point was for centuries one of the most famous in England, and certainly the most often painted: a silver river crossing a green quilt of trees and fields, enlivened by the white façades of houses. The eighteenth-century German traveller Carl Moritz wrote that it was 'in its kind the purest and loveliest natural prospect I have ever witnessed'. Nobody disagreed. Here in 1772 the leading artist of the day, Sir Joshua Reynolds, ordered the architect Sir William Chambers to build him a mansion and studio. He was moved to produce a rare landscape, *Petersham and Twickenham Meadows*, full of the gentle light of the Thames in summer.

The view has changed little since then – and will have changed even less when one day the distant gasholders and tower blocks are pulled down. The Thames still snakes away towards Hampton and trees helpfully conceal suburban roofs. But this is not a scene entirely of good manners. I remember one evening watching the sun sinking towards the Berkshire horizon. Ham and Marble Hill were disappearing into twilight and the Thames was turning from silver to grey. When all trace of day seemed gone, the sun suddenly appeared from beneath a cloud and fired the river into a trough of flame. The effect was extraordinary. The scene was instantly transformed into a surreal tableau, where monarchs fled from avaricious courtiers; where Henry VIII plotted against his Chancellors and murdered his wives; where Charles I's cavaliers made a last desperate thrust towards London; where Hanoverians banished each other from court. It was a river of blood in a landscape of nobility, Burns's liquid history.

The towpath now leads under the lee of the hill towards the bustle of Richmond waterfront. With the sun shining, this might almost be the quay of a South Coast fishing town. Yachts and motor boats are moored two or three abreast. Pleasure boats take tourists up and downstream. Pubs spill over on to the bank. At centre stage is Richmond Bridge, built in 1777 and now the oldest on the tidal Thames. It is, with Albert Bridge in Chelsea, one of the few London river crossings that are not mere projections of roads but spring to life from each bank in an ellipse. The town of Richmond lost its heart when the Tudor palace, Queen Elizabeth's favourite, was demolished soon after her death. Its surviving ranges were converted to houses and its jousting ground became the present Green. Tudor fragments can still be seen facing the Green. Maids of Honour Row is a handsome early eighteenth-century terrace. The Maids of Honour were those of the future George II, whose banishment from court by his father instantly made Kew and Richmond resorts of fashion. The Row is most pleasing to the eye, its doorcases, redbrick and white dressings and climbing vegetation memorials to a vanished craft of Georgian townscape.

Before we reach the Green, we pass the new Richmond riverfront. The town's recent history has been dominated by the politics of preservation, in particular the fate of the ugly rear elevations of buildings along Hill Street backing on to the river. Should they be rebuilt piecemeal, or might the whole town be turned inside out and given a new focus? For any community to design itself a new town centre would be a moment of importance. For Richmond it caused an identity crisis. Should the new development be ancient or modern, garish or restrained, offices or lawns? Should there be one architect or many, one developer or many, public or private? The outcome was no compromise but a total victory for traditionalism. One architect was given his head, the classicist Quinlan Terry. He produced a group of neo-Georgian façades set as a backdrop to terraced lawns leading down to the river, almost like the Backs at Cambridge. The effect is of a stage set with the river as audience.

Terry's Richmond riverfront is truly reactionary modern architecture: a pavilion here, a Renaissance façade there, a bit of Regency, a bit of Palladio, all set above a grass slope and with the bridge and water as an integral part of the composition. I find it impossible to walk it in company without plunging into argument over its virtues and vices. Is it not absurd to 'create' informality? Is it honest to present new as if it were old, a set of uniform commercial interiors as if they had developed hotchpotch over decades? The straight answer is, 'Imagine the alternatives. Look at the thudding jackboot of Croydon's town centre or the horrors of modern Kingston just up the river.' Is this not preferable? I think so. But Terry's design leaves me uneasy. It looks like the Old Guard punishing London for a quarter-century of infidelity to the true faith, a reversion to the status quo ante, not a bold step forward. Yet Richmond riverfront is immensely popular and always crowded with people, the true vote of confidence in an architect.

Richmond is quickly left behind. Tucked under the railway bridge is Asgill House, a Palladian weekend retreat for a Lord Mayor of London built by Sir Robert Taylor in 1758. A coade stone head of Father Thames looks out over the river above a ground-floor French window. From here the towpath re-enters country past a quaint Victorian sluice used to keep Richmond's boats, and its daring band of swimmers, afloat at low tide. For the next two and a half miles we amble along a secluded track running beneath trees past the Old Deer Park and Kew Gardens. On the opposite bank are Isleworth, Syon and Brentford. Apart from the tower blocks of Brentford, there is little to remind us of the twentieth century. Isleworth and its famous pub, the London Apprentice, are by this stage of the walk tantalizingly inaccessible. Next come the ancient Tudor walls of Syon Park, seen across meadows and a pleasantly unkempt riverbank. The view from the Kew bank to Syon, home of the Dukes of Northumberland and often painted by Richard Wilson and others, is unchanged over centuries. A royal park looks across at a ducal one. Monarchs may come and go, the Old Deer Park may have become a golf course and Kew a museum. But His Grace the Duke is still ensconced in Syon. The house, with its Adam interiors, is out of reach of this walk. But its unspoilt gardens and park, designed by Capability Brown, can be appreciated in tranquillity from afar.

At Brentford the Grand Union Canal enters the Thames in a mess of wharves and industrial development. You could take a boat from here to Limehouse and the Docks by way of Southall, Maida Vale, Camden Town, Islington and Mile End Road. The voyage would take in London's most exotic fraternity, the St Pancras Yacht Club. It would occupy at least three days, but must be the only cross-town route completely free of traffic and noise, a secret passage through the city's Victorian archaeology. (Almost as antique is the old Richmond 'magic railway' that follows a roughly similar route from Richmond Station along the North London Line to Liverpool Street.)

Now at the journey's end, the river seems to widen and mature. Its reaches fill the vistas up and downstream. Water birds are plentiful and oarsmen skim back and forth on its surface. The scene is always peaceful. The feet are weary and no sight is as welcome as that of Kew Bridge ahead.

12

THE NOBLEST
NATIONALIZATION

WE MANAGED it well. When they write the history of twentieth-century Britain, they must not forget what we did right. With painstaking care, we removed hundreds of the greatest houses in the land from the ownership of distressed private citizens into a sympathetic public domain. A century ago, the English landscape could be traversed on a Grand Tour of cultural history. From Knole to Hardwick, from Kedleston to St Michael's Mount, from Hadrian's Wall to Land's End, the nation's ancestral art and architecture were largely extant and on display. Two world wars and a social revolution later, that display is still with us, almost intact.

How was it done? No government ordained this success. No Napoleonic edict went out. The task was written in no manifesto. Since the mid-1930s, a small band of enthusiasts took it upon themselves to induce first a handful, then dozens, then hundreds of grandees to part with houses and estates that had been in their families for generations. Civil servants and politicians played at most a small role in this. The cost, mostly in tax relief, was minimal. The trick was one of masterly confidence.

James Lees-Milne was the greatest of these tricksters. His diary of a genteel but cultured life is already on the bedside table. His most recent book, *People and Places*, written at the age of 84, is a different sort of record. It tells the story of the Trust's first country house acquisitions. Apart from the pleasure of the writing, the book is a manual of sensitive administration. It should be read by every legislator, bureaucrat and centralizer in the land, a classic of 'alternative' public service.

Lees-Milne was the first country house secretary of the National Trust, appointed in 1936 at the age of 27. The Trust then had a staff of just half a dozen and was chiefly concerned with protecting parcels of attractive countryside. Its leadership decided to dip its toe into the country house business only on finding many owners facing unsustainable death duties after the Great War. On top of the agricultural recession, these duties presented many families with a ghastly choice: either to pull down their houses or to sell them and flee. Even the latter often meant separation not just of family from estate but of land from house. This plight was not high on any political agenda. All the Trust could offer owners in return for a house and its land was continued tenancy, a promise of love and attention and, from 1937, relief from death duties. Lees-Milne was appointed to sell this policy to the distressed nobility and gentry of England.

His book is a case history of fourteen of the early negotiations. They brought to the Trust the most magnificent portfolio of monuments anywhere in Europe. They also made Lees-Milne privy to the innermost secrets of such ornate families as the Sackvilles, the Lothians, the Dashwoods and the Trevelyans. The story begins as a sad afterword to the much-lamented 'twilight of the English aristocracy'. After the twilight had come night: war and depression, death and taxes. These families were the unlucky ones. 'The estate is mildly embarrassed,' the Earl would tell Lees-Milne gloomily over a brandy, his wife sobbing in the background. The son had fallen at the Somme. Developers and auctioneers were circling overhead. Socialism was at the door. With the outbreak of another war in 1939 came a new menace. A defence ministry of extraordinary philistinism burst in, evicting, requisitioning, altering and smashing everything. 'Don't you know there's a war on?' was the excuse for such vandalism. Some of these houses had survived every war since Agincourt.

Over the horizon would pedal young Lees-Milne, Eton and Magdalen, on a bicycle from the nearest station. He is no civil servant.

He has no rule book or uniform or quartermaster sergeant at his elbow. He seems to know the house already. He enthuses over it. He admires the pictures. He reassuringly mentions a schoolfriend in common. He is polite to the servants. In his bag is not gold, but enough base metal to offer a sort of salvation: tax relief, a custodianship agreement, a small repair carried out, advice on restoration, above all, respect and dignity preserved.

The agony of these people is as palpable as their eccentricity. At Attingham, Lord Berwick still has stabling for sixty horses and a conviction that his vacuum-cleaner is a ghost. He invites Lees-Milne down to negotiate but is too humiliated to talk. Conversation passes through the wife. She and Lees-Milne walk in circles round the old man as he murmurs, 'Not an acre shall be sold.' At Brockhampton, seat of the Lutleys for 750 years, the bachelor Colonel Lutley is suddenly appalled at what he is doing to the shades of his ancestors. Lees-Milne has to retreat to a pub.

At Stourhead the Hoares remain unaware of the full implication of what they have agreed, even after transfer is complete. They treat the National Trust as no more than an employment agency. At the height of the war they write to ask the Trust for 'some evacuees who know how to polish silver with peacock feathers'. At Cotehele Lees-Milne is negotiating the acquisition of the house with its owner, Lady Mount Edgcombe, when he sees her puppy munching its way through the house's most valuable asset, the Queen Anne needlework. 'You naughty thing,' she scolds as each priceless inch disappears. Lees-Milne dare not risk offence. Next he is invited to witness the dying rituals of Lacock Abbey, where the last Miss Talbot keeps up local spirits with a desperate Christmas dance. 'Plain, speechless girls' gaze at a wind-up gramophone while a yule log fills the room with smoke and fog swirls against the Gothick windows.

Lyme Park in Cheshire has been in the Legh family, Lords Newton, since 1388. Sir Piers Legh served at Crécy. The family have occupied the house in unbroken succession for nearly six hundred years. The old Tudor mansion was not demolished but carefully extended in the eighteenth century, to achieve what Lees-Milne regards as 'one of the boldest achievements of English Palladian architecture' to survive anywhere in England. The deer park runs for 1,300 acres to the edge of the Pennines. Here were bred the famous Lyme mastiffs, dogs the size of ponies. When Lees-Milne arrives he finds the Newtons in the depths of gloom, moving about their doomed inheritance 'sighing from noon to night'. No less sad is Hanbury in Worcestershire, a perfect Squire Western house of 1701. It is not grand, despite its Thornhill murals, and by 1938 it is devoid of hope. Lady Vernon is 'down to two rooms and one maid'. Lees-Milne discovers her surrounded by vast cats, eating queen's pudding and whispering to him her one state secret, 'Droitwich is getting very queer these days.'

At such moments, most public officials would run for the door and send the local solicitor a form in triplicate. Lees-Milne smiles tolerantly, meeting self-pity with sympathy. Following the acquisition of Smallhythe in Kent the previous owner, Ellen Terry's daughter, and her friends are allowed to stay as custodians. They refuse to submit paperwork to account for their new role on the grounds that 'We thought the National Trust was civilized.' This is a serious breach of the rules, but Lees-Milne pleads their cause with his superiors. Every house must be kept occupied, if possible with those who know it and will love and care for it. Rules may have to be bent – occupants may sometimes prove barking mad – but so be it. The need for sensitive conservation is greater than any rulebook.

I believe Lees-Milne is here stating some fundamental truths about all public administration, not just the custodianship of historic houses. His approach was based not on organization and authority but on simple trust between individuals. It is administration *ad hominem*. Each deal was fragile. In less sensitive hands all these negotiations might have foundered. Without trust, owners would have despaired and handed their estates over to the auction houses, the ever-present vultures of the tale. Certainly they would have done that before ceding them to any agency of Whitehall. In return for winning tax relief from the Treasury, the National Trust took upon itself heavy obligations. It had to acquire ownership of long-settled estates, a complicated business. It had to ensure that the buildings were maintained, that the estates were properly run, that there was no fraud, that the houses were in most cases open to the public. In return it could offer the owners only a tenancy, and the unquantifiable benefits of genteel treatment and continued association with the property. It is hard to imagine a relationship more vulnerable to bruised feelings, bloody-mindedness and eventual collapse.

There was more to the National Trust's success than its policy of minimum intervention and a willingness to bend rules (not bend them far enough, say some modern occupants). The policy could not have worked without the specific people who ran it. What emerges from Lees-Milne's account is the importance of touch. He and his colleagues worked by knowing when to leave well alone, when to delegate. They used nepotism, a call to a friend, a leaning on the great and good, a knowing when to lean and when not to lean. It was the finest hour of the old-boy network. Only thus was mighty Knole prized from the Sackvilles. Only thus was the air ministry repulsed from Blickling.

I believe the aristocracy of Britain yielded up its finest possessions because it rightly believed it was yielding them into the care of like-minded guardians. It was the apotheosis of true Conservative leadership, an instinct for ruling rather than an ideology of government. Certainly it seems far from the practice of today's ever more centralist public administration. Trust officials were manifestly of the same class and stock as those with whom they dealt. They did not change each year. They shared assumptions, friends, even families. They knew how to sympathize with great families in their hour of sorrow. Government played its part. It gave the Trust what it most wanted when it needed it, tax relief. But it was enabler rather than executive. It delegated policy to a body which it too could trust and which honoured that trust. I can think of no more admirable model for modern administration. Since Lees-Milne began his work, 300 of the finest houses in Britain have been saved and put on public display. They will not readily be threatened again.

13

THE CULT OF THE RUIN

THE POLLUTION of Athens has taken a day off. It is midwinter and a vivid sun is setting over the Bay of Phaleron, dusting pink the marble of the Acropolis. A lone group of Japanese tourists keeps watch. The Athenian gods are back on form. But which gods? Those of the Classical city or new gods, those of modern archaeology?

In December 1987 the Greek arts minister, Melina Mercouri, declared 'open' the Erechtheum temple after an eight-year £1m restoration programme. The rest of the Acropolis monuments are due to follow, including the Parthenon. The Erechtheum is for many visitors the supreme Acropolis shrine. The site was probably that of the earliest temple on the rock, dedicated to the three founding deities of Athens, Athena, Poseidon and Erechtheus. The last was the son of Hephaestos and the Earth. The Earth was said to have put him in a chest and handed him to Athena. Her acolytes, on finding that he was shaped like a serpent, went mad and threw themselves off the Acropolis to their deaths. The first temple was burnt by the Persians. The present one was constructed, probably by Mnesicles under the direction of Pericles, in the fifth century BC. Since then it has been a Christian church, a Turkish harem and a squatter's hut.

What we see today is what I can only term a 'designer ruin'. Were Athena's acolytes to return, they would have hysterics all over again. The new Erechtheum, with its gaping roof and three fractured porches, including that of the caryatids, is a patent absurdity. If ever there were an example of conservation by committee, this is it. The temple has been stripped of any encrustation that might suggest the passing of time. Yet the opportunity to reconstruct the complete Periclean temple as we know it to have been has been passed up. The architect of the ruin, Alexandros Papanicolaou, has fallen between two stools. He has rebuilt the walls more or less to the level of the last restoration, but he has stopped short of the roof. Gaps in the original structure have been filled with new marble, but cut to make it visually distinct from the old. The juxtaposition is ugly.

I have some sympathy with Papanicolaou. The Greeks have been criticized as poor guardians of the Acropolis treasures. Before the Second World War, they cut up the original marble blocks of which the temples were made and inserted ungalvanized iron clamps to hold them in place. These rusted and split the stone. Athens's lax city authorities allowed sulphur dioxide pollution to turn the original Pantelic marble to pumice. To see some of this marble today – carved by the finest craftsmen ever to set hand to chisel – is like seeing the paint of an old master blistering under a torch. As long as this pollution continues, the Trustees of the British Museum can easily dismiss pleas that the Elgin marbles be returned to such filthy air.

In 1975, when the Acropolis seemed to be suffering from galloping decomposition, Athens determined to make its rescue the symbol of Greek intellectual and archaeological revival. A new industry was born. Where once Franks, Turks and Venetians laid siege to the Acropolis, it is now invested by laboratories, computer facilities, drawing offices, foundries, washing, moulding and casting rooms. Experts from around the world gaze at each grain of ancient marble as a winemaster might examine a grape. They do not care that much of the Acropolis looks like a down-at-heel mason's yard. Archaeologists and architects can seize one of the world's most popular sites for as long as they like. They are the new masters of the Acropolis and have their own priorities.

The Greek authorities decided that not a stone would be touched, let alone moved or replaced, without a stamp of approval from the great and good of world Hellenism. An international

Committee for the Restoration of the Acropolis Monuments was formed and consulted at every turn. There would be no arguments or jealousies. The conservers' bible, the 1964 Charter of Venice, would be obeyed to the letter. Every fragment of the temples was X-rayed, mapped, seismographed, chemically analysed and its locational history charted. Ruins would be 'conserved as found'. There was to be none of the total or partial reconstruction fashionable in the nineteenth century or between the wars. Any restoration must be distinguishable, new from old, and inserted so as to be reversible by future generations. Viewers should know precisely what they were seeing. They should be able to read a wall like an archaeology textbook, with each layer marked and evident.

The protocols of the Venice Charter had been drawn up in reaction to the excesses of the previous century. They were a commendable discipline, especially in countries with weak conservation laws and facing hard choices on restoration. But like most protocols, they could be nonsensical if implemented without discretion. The new Erechtheum is a case in point. An archaeological jigsaw puzzle has been taken to pieces and reassembled, with rust-free titanium rods to hold it together. No expense has been spared. The question confronting Papanicolaou was bound to be contentious: how many original stones should be to hand before any reconstruction of a wall or frieze was 'justified'? Where it was justified, how should patching be handled in those stretches of the structure where not every stone was extant? Should he treat it as a restorer might a medieval church or a Georgian house, making the new a counterfeit of the old? Or should he conform to the letter of the Venice Charter and make its newness obtrusive?

Papanicolaou mostly chose the latter course. For instance, enough fragments of the Erechtheum pediment were to hand to permit a partial reconstruction, but not quite enough to give it a sense of balance. Some fragments have therefore been recarved to give an 'impression' of the completed outline, but without actually completing it. A pillar has been installed where missing, again in the interest of balance, but it has been made of concrete – which spoils the balance. New marble has been used to fill holes in walls and patch severely eroded blocks. Papanicolaou, or the committee, appears to feel that new marble is appropriate for structural features but not for carved ones. Yet in some places new marble has been cut, in others the eroded blocks have been left in place. The result is that some corners have been finished and look pristine, others are left jagged.

Nothing is more cruel than the fate visited on the severely eroded caryatid maidens. These have been removed from the polluted open air and placed in the adjacent Acropolis Museum. They have been replaced neither by marble copies of the existing, eroded statues nor by newly carved statues of the maidens as they would have been when new. Instead they have been replaced with concrete casts of the eroded versions. The Acropolis workshops have computerized jigs capable of recarving any caryatid, new or eroded, in marble from the original quarries. Yet such recarving was considered 'deceptive', academically impure, and against the Charter ideology. Instead we have pastiches of eroded statues in an ugly modern material. They now commemorate not the glory of the Acropolis but one of the worse moments in its history, when it was all but destroyed by atmospheric pollution. To add insult to injury, these new casts are resting on partly new plinths carved from the same 'deceptive' marble that was not allowed for the statues themselves. Never has academic discipline so obviously achieved the worst of all worlds.

Lest Britons grow smug at this, they should reflect on their own part in this fiasco: the removal of one caryatid and one column from the east portico by Lord Elgin. Both are now in the British Museum. Even apologists for the removal of the Parthenon marbles found the taking of the Erechtheum column and caryatid (later replaced by a cast) hard to defend. Given the subsequent erosion of the Acropolis, their sojourn in Bloomsbury has undoubtedly been fortunate. Now that the surviving caryatids are in a group in the clean air of the Acropolis Museum, there must be a good case for returning the missing one. If nothing else, it would show the Athens authorities what years of neglect have done to the rest of their Acropolis heritage. In my view, the Greeks should have carved new statues in marble and erected them on site, sealed against pollution. But this opportunity was missed. London can at least boast a copy of the complete portico, attached to the north wall of St Pancras New Church opposite Euston.

If the Greeks hoped that their deference to international archaeology would spare them controversy, they were disappointed. Anywhere as sensitive as the Acropolis was bound to open academic
wounds. No sooner had Miss Mercouri opened the new Erechtheum than a former director of the Acropolis, George Dontas,
accused his successors (via the London *Times*) of going too far in
what he called 'intervention'. He accused them of the cardinal
archaeological crime, that of zeal. They were adulterating the evidence of the past in their eagerness to show off their brilliance.
To archaeologists of Mr Dontas's generation, schooled to abhor
Victorian and Edwardian reconstructions, any rebuilding, even
one as tentative as that of the Erechtheum, induces horror. Any
intervention is a step down the road to destruction.

This attitude of mind, while understandable, leads to a barren
pedantry. An example of it was the treatment of British ruins by
the Ministry of Public Building and Works after the war. The
stabilization programme yielded a series of 'tended ruins', scholastically respectable but visually unexciting. Later building on or
around 'true' ruins was cleared, vegetation was stripped away and
footings marked out with concrete. (There was even a proposal to
destroy the Georgian houses built into the medieval arches of Bury
St Edmunds Abbey.) Such ruins do not possess the picturesque
accretions of time. Nor do they recall the appearance of the original. They are like municipal gardens, with neat lawns, scrubbed
stones and clipped edges. These sites may have meaning for the
cognoscenti but not for the public. They are repositories of learning, libraries for scholars; they are not evocative reminders of the
past.

Every age restores the past to its own taste. Yet what is the
alternative, if not to let every historic building crumble to dust?
At Knossos we gaze in awe at Sir Arthur Evans's interwar 'Minoan'
palaces and 'Minoan' princesses. We dream ourselves back 3,000
years even if the content of that dream owes more to Sir Arthur
than to Knossos. At Carcassonne we marvel at a medieval fortress
town, knowing that it is mostly the imagination of Viollet-le-Duc
in 1844. At Chartres and Rheims we study modern replicas in the
statue niches and feel we are being given an admission ticket to
early Gothic art. We hug the Romanesque pillars of Durham and

do not worry that what we hug was carved in the last century. The campanile in St Mark's Square is a structure of 1902. We do not feel conned by this. We still photograph it. The Temple of Concord at Agrigento is heavy with restorer's concrete. The fifteenth-century façade of Magdalen College, Oxford, should strictly speaking be dated as *circa* 1981. However 'untrue' these monuments, they retain the power to send our imagination back down the road of time. Restored, they still convey their message. They remain Keats's rosy sanctuary 'adorned with the wreathed trellis of a working brain'.

Most of these sites would be more sensitively reconstituted today. Even so, I would not want Knossos reduced back to its original foundations. Evans's work conveys his own informed understanding of Minoan culture. It is more evocative than, for instance, neighbouring Phaestos though it is certainly less authentic. I would not tear the Victorian dressings from an Early English church or rip off the nineteenth-century additions of the Tower of London for the purity of its Norman keep. Great buildings live on through the imagination of those who seek to return to them some of the meaning that time destroys. We restore Georgian buildings as near as we can to their eighteenth-century appearance. We labour over Old Masters to keep alive some of their original freshness. We do so with great care and great scholarship. We may make mistakes. But not to try, to leave the past to decay, is as irresponsible as it is pedantic. If there is a moral duty at stake, it is surely to pass the relics of the past on in good order to the future.

At the foot of the Acropolis is the Centre for Acropolis Studies, with a display of restoration work across the whole of the site. Here we are introduced to the greatest challenge of all, the Parthenon. In charge is a young architect still in his thirties, Manolis Korres. He and his team have amassed 75 per cent of the fragments of the Parthenon's eastern colonnade. Some would consider this more than enough to justify its reconstruction. This is the colonnade that was demolished in the devastating Venetian siege of 1687, when a Turkish powder store in the Parthenon was hit by a shell and exploded. The stones scattered across the Acropolis and later found their way into buildings throughout the city. Once reconstructed, the colonnade could even be crowned with casts of the relevant friezes now in the British Museum.

To start reconstructing any of the pre-explosion Parthenon is to cross an archaeological Rubicon. Korres is preparing a 700-page report for the international committee, at which the full weight of academic scepticism will descend on him. Yet his proposal is modest alongside the sort of reconstruction that is now feasible. The Acropolis team must now know (almost) everything that is likely to be known about the Parthenon. They have its exact dimensions. They have scoured Athens and the world's museums for every available or copyable fragment of even the smallest feature. They have pieces of the pre-explosion walls, roofs, even roof tiles. In Nashville, Tennessee, is a concrete reconstruction of 1922 based on prewar measuring and copying, including plaster casts of the Elgin marbles. Such has been the subsequent erosion that the Tennesseeans boast the Greeks would need to come to them for details of many features. All this has been done.

The purist says that we can never know what the original Parthenon was really like. We cannot recreate the gilding or the colours. We cannot repeat the artistry of the frieze or the majesty of Phidias' statue of Athena. We know nothing for sure and should therefore be humble. But humble before whom? Which gods are we here propitiating? The cult of the ruin has its place in the experience of past civilizations. The picturesque quality of many ruins is intense and often moving. In her book *Pleasure of Ruins*, Rose Macaulay described the ruin-hunter as experiencing 'an intoxication at once so heady and so devout: it is not the romantic melancholy engendered by broken towers and mouldering stones; it is the soaring of the imagination into the high empyrean where huge episodes are tangled with myths and dreams.' Macaulay accepted what Henry James called the heartlessness, even 'the note of perversity' in the pursuit of ruins. It was, she said, a half-mystical encounter with the 'extant fragments of some lost and noble poem'.

Yet we are not dealing here in ghosts but in the custody of a building and its history. There is no lack of shrines at which the cult may worship. My point is that these shrines are peculiar. Ruins are as transient as the structures of which they are shadows. Macaulay complained that her favourite ruins were changing so fast it was hard to keep pace with them. 'One must select for contemplation', she wrote, 'some phase in a ruin's devious career, it matters little which.' But it does matter to the conservationist. Every intervention, to stabilize or to restore, is an arbitrary act. And while there will always be ruins, there are few reconstructed buildings from antiquity that convey some of the spirit of their creation.

The masters of the Acropolis do not claim to be displaying tended ruins. They claim to be displaying what the tourist brochure calls 'The glory that was Periclean Athens'. Is that glory nothing but broken stones? The idea of leaving ruins alone is disregarded for modern buildings. We do not condemn burnt-out Windsor Castle or Hampton Court to Macaulay's 'romantic melancholy'. We restore any structural decay in an old building with alacrity. Yet we accept without question the concept of the ruin for Classical remains. This is indeed a Jamesian perversity. I would not wish to reconstruct the mass of Classical ruins littered round the Mediterranean. We have neither the knowledge nor the money to do so. But I do believe the task of communicating the past to the future requires greater boldness in the matter of restoration.

This need be no more than a matter of common sense. There is much wisdom in the Venice Charter. Restoration should be undertaken only with caution and skill. Any intervention should be non-destructive. It must be for our time not for all time. It should be documented and made reversible. Yet scholarship has given us the knowledge and science has given us the means to rebuild many of Pericles' masterpieces, should we want to do so. We can respect the character of the original, respect its form, shape and detail. We can clone each architectural fragment and cut them from the same marble strains in the original quarries. All that would be lost is a ruin, the arbitrary creation of the trajectory of a Venetian bomb. The Erechtheum compromise would be avoided. A monument to Greek scholarship and craftsmanship, ancient and modern, would be restored to a sort of life.

Such a proposal does not come from Korres nor, to the best of my knowledge, from any archaeologist. To them it is still anathema. Ruins must be appreciated as ruins, for their own sake. Whatever the Parthenon may once have been, for three centuries it has

111

been the world's most celebrated wreck. Yet I believe the time has come to consider its reconstruction. This is not a matter of truth to history. The new Erechtheum is not true. The only truth to history would be total disengagement, leaving these great buildings to degenerate and collapse. This is more a matter of taste. Anything we do to the Acropolis is done by the present for the future. (These ruins are being held in place by titanium rods: reconstruction would obviate such modern solecisms.) Rebuilding would conform to the intentions of the original architect and make his message clear to a contemporary public. I am sure the Athenians of old would laugh if they could listen to the deliberations of the Acropolis committee.

Below the Acropolis in the former Athenian agora, on the far side from the Centre, is an apparently modern rectangular structure. It is a replica made by the American archaeologist Homer Thompson in 1956 of the old market colonnade, the Stoa of Attalus. It includes fragments of the original and is in immaculate Pantelic marble. It looks not at all like today's idea of what an Athenian market place should be – which is as a ruin. Yet an Athenian market was not a ruin. It was not a pile of rubble but a roofed building in which Athenians did their daily business. When it needed repair, it was repaired. The shock we feel at being confronted by a three-dimensional example of what the past was really like is a stark instance of our cultural conditioning. We are shocked because we have been told to be shocked. Our imagination, our understanding of the past, has suffered a distortion. The past has been formed in our minds not as it was but as a blighted desert filled with ruins.

I believe future generations will come to see the reconstructed Stoa as closer to the spirit of ancient Athens than the ruins hovering above. If the Stoa, they will say, why not the Parthenon? How liberating it would be if our vision of the past could free itself from the cult of the ruin, if one of greatest Periclean monuments could be revealed in its original glory: a majestic, garish celebration of the gods that inspired its creation. Antagonism to such reconstruction is perverse. Lulled by an affection for the picturesque, we appear afraid of the past, as if deliberately wishing to shut out aspects of it that might disturb received wisdom.

Plutarch visited the Acropolis in the first century AD and mar-
velled at what he saw. The temples, he said, possessed 'a bloom
. . . which preserves their aspect untarnished by time, as if they
were animated with a spirit of perpetual youth'.

Today Plutarch would find none of that youthful magic. He
would be baffled at the respect shown by the twentieth century to
the mere ruin of a great civilization. He would ask why? He would
be referred to a committee. But in years to come, perhaps not for
a century, I am sure somebody will have the courage to rebuild.
They will give Pericles back his glory. They will say with Shelley,

> Another Athens shall arise,
> And to remoter time
> Bequeath, like sunset to the skies,
> The splendour of its prime.

14

DEATH ON THE NILE

I met a traveller from an antique land
Who said: 'Two vast and trunkless legs of stone
Stand in the desert. Near them on the sand,
Half sunk, a shattered visage lies . . .'

NOT FOR long it didn't. Shelley's lines on Ozymandias were stimulated by the Regency excavator turned impresario, Giovanni Belzoni. In 1816 Belzoni had dragged a huge bust of Rameses II from Luxor to London for public display. The bust now stands in the British Museum's Egyptian gallery. 'Nothing beside remains,' continued Shelley, who had never visited Luxor. He was wrong. The bust's torso, snapped off at the chest, is still there in the sand. Its twin lies next to it, relic of another decapitation. Behind rises not Shelley's 'lone and level sands' but the Ramesseum temple, one of the finest in Egypt. Behind that in turn rise the hills of the Valley of the Kings, where in 1922 Howard Carter discovered the tomb of Tutankhamun.

To visit the monuments of the Upper Nile today is moving but sad. They greet the winter tourist with gap-toothed smiles. The gaps are not just those of age, great though that is, but of a single century (the nineteenth) in which the monuments were smashed and stripped to fill the museums of the world. The removals have ceased. The gaps remain and the local guidebooks tell a doleful tale of where the scattered fragments have come to rest.

As long ago as 1836, the temple of Luxor saw one of its two entrance obelisks, the last pair standing in Egypt, torn out to adorn the Place de la Concorde in Paris. The Paris obelisk had been demanded 'as a gift' of the local pasha by the French archaeologist, Champollion. At the beginning of this century the obelisk enthusiast Wallis Budge remarked that to remove one of the pair (demolishing many houses in the process) 'was as many writers have justly said a gross act of vandalism. How the French government can have sanctioned such a thing . . . is not easily understood.' Its pair remains in place, lopsiding the symmetry of the building. The approach to an Egyptian temple is supposedly a procession of balanced architectural proportion. Today Luxor lies askew, like an old elephant with one tusk torn out by poachers. There is no good reason for the French not to return the obelisk and erect a copy in its place in Paris.

Britain has behaved no better. A mile downstream at Karnak, the king Amenophis III is represented by his legs alone. The rest of his anatomy is dispersed, with his head, arms and fist in the British Museum. At Philae above Aswan, the Ptolemies created an island temple to Isis, a jewel of antique architecture. When the temple had to be moved to an adjacent higher island in the 1970s to avoid the rising water level, nobody thought to return its obelisk taken by Belzoni in 1815. It had survived in the dry heat of the desert since 300 BC; it is now eroding in the rain at Kingston Lacy in Dorset, to whose antiquarian owner, W.J. Bankes, Belzoni sold it. Philae is now visited by hundreds of thousands a year. (Its *son et lumière*, spoken by British actors, is without equal.) That so crucial a part of its architectural setting should be decaying in Britain is an outrage.

There is at Karnak a sanctuary to Sekhmet, the lion-headed goddess. The granite images of the goddess have vanished and tourists pass by unmoved. The better informed ones learn, however, that the statues that used to occupy the empty plinths are not lost. They are sitting on a gloomy British Museum landing in Bloomsbury, shared with a fire extinguisher, a wooden doorcase and a Tannoy. They have neither context nor dignity. I doubt if

one user of the staircase in a hundred even looks at them. There is
no excuse for this incongruity. It is an offence against art, national
identity and, I suppose, religion. Here is a museum saying simply,
what we have we hold. No argument, no money, no power on
earth is going to take it from us. We intend to keep these things
for ever. (Or so it was once put to me by a British Museum trustee.)

I do not believe that this line can be held. We shall shortly
see a new chapter in archaeological diplomacy. For the past two
centuries, explorers, excavators and thieves could claim with justice that some countries were unable to excavate or conserve the
relics of their past. Once discovered, these relics would be lost if
they were not removed to the safe keeping of European museums.
Taking was conserving. In the case of Egypt, Ottoman officials
had little interest in the history of this corner of their empire. Their
concern was to prevent Anglo-French rivalry from becoming a
nuisance. Money talked and wealthy collectors either bribed to
gain permits or simply bought monuments on the open market. It
was seldom necesssary to steal. Even Unesco, when it pondered
cultural 'restitution' in 1970, called for the return only of artefacts
that had not been legitimately acquired. It thus sidestepped vexed
cases such as the Elgin marbles, the Maori skulls and the Ashanti
regalia – objects removed by conquest, imperial pre-emption,
bribery or simple purchase.

Soon these niceties of legal title will be brushed aside. Newly
assertive nations develop a regard for their past, partly from a
reborn nationalism, partly from a need to exploit tourism. They
may take their case to international appeal at Unesco, the Council
of Europe or the European Community (whose members hold the
lion's share of the spoils). Or they may negotiate bilaterally
through diplomatic channels, threatening such retaliation as they
can muster, as Greece does periodically over the Elgin marbles.
These are not matters to be resolved by law or by museum claims
that 'what we hold we own'. The return of the treasures of Mesopo-
tamia and the Nile will be demanded by peoples rediscovering
their national identity. They will see in these monuments their
one-time gift to civilization. That the gift was taken, however
legally, to a foreign land is a reminder of their impotence. Their
power may have declined and that of Europe risen. But that history

is past. These countries will want to negotiate restitution. They will not accept that their treasures are lost to them for ever.

Already the worm is starting to turn. The Hungarian crown jewels have been sent back from America to Hungary. King Priam's treasure is being returned from Moscow to Berlin, from where it was stolen during the war. One day it should go from Berlin back to Troy, where Schliemann originally plundered it. States in the former Dutch East Indies are seeking ancestral relics back from the Netherlands. The Maoris are combing the world for similar relics. At the same time, some of the old arguments against restitution are weakening. Museum curators once claimed that the treasures of the Nile were not only better conserved in London, but the world could more easily visit and study them there. This is no longer the case. In time, more people will be admiring the temples of Luxor in Luxor than will take an equivalent interest in the broken fragments of them in London. Mass tourism and television have made the sites of the Nile accessible to millions.

Conservators remain sceptical of the ability of some countries to look after restituted monuments. That is presumably a temporary rather than permanent objection. Many small countries have excellent museums, aided by institutions such as the British Museum in London. The sites of the Nile valley are being restored through an extensive international programme. Since the rescue of the Nubian temples in the 1960s, this programme has become a great enterprise of archaeological co-operation. Nobody now suggests that relics should be removed from Egypt for safe keeping. Archaeologists rightly believe that the most helpful conservation lies in advice and aid direct to the sites and museums in the countries concerned.

Yet if this is so, how odd to deny the possibility of putting back into the expensively restored temples architectural features known to be located in museums abroad. The argument is particularly weak in the case of obelisks. The Egyptian atmosphere, away from Cairo, is far cleaner and drier than the fume-ridden traffic arteries of London, Paris, Rome and New York. Conservation alone demands their immediate return. Cleopatra's needle, which reached London in 1877 after its transporter was thought lost in the Bay of Biscay, was deliberately left uncovered during the Blitz.

The government claimed that a few shrapnel scars would add to its patina of antiquity. Such was the attitude of those who said they were 'removing to conserve'.

The craft of facsimile also is sufficiently advanced to be a factor in the debate. The Italians are copying more and more of their open air statuary to protect it from pollution. Most tourists are unaware of this. Venice's bronze horses on the façade of St Mark's are made of non-corroding glass-fibre. The originals are in a museum. Michelangelo's *David*, photographed by thousands each day outside the Palazzo Vecchio in Florence, is a replica. The Romanesque carvings taken to the Cloisters Museum in Manhattan have been replaced in France with carved facsimiles. Why the facsimiles could not have been put in New York and the originals left in peace is not clear. Some might suggest that the countries of origin should make their own replicas. Certainly this would be cheaper. But it would not meet the nationalist complaint, loudest with 'crown jewel' restitution, that the act of removal was the insult and that it must be reversed. The object carries a symbolic significance that a facsimile can never replicate. If Britain's state treasures lost in the Civil War were to reappear in some foreign museum, no plaster copies would do. We would want the real thing.

Museums themselves can make copies of objects that they regard as scholastically important to their collections. There is nothing new in the concept of a copy. Until the middle of this century, museums were commonly filled with reproductions of works in other museums, notably casts of statues. American galleries were proud of their cast collections, regarding their primary task as to secure the widest access for the public to works of art, but not necessarily original ones. This approach changed when museums came to see themselves more as treasure troves of rare and costly objects. Copies and casts became anathema, symbols of curatorial poverty. Boston Museum controversially destroyed hundreds of casts from its collection.

I believe that this anathema will lift. Video screens and other forms of reproduction play an ever larger part in museum interpretation. Copies and casts will do so too – albeit over the dead bodies of some curators. This diversity should make it easier for museums and their public to be open-minded on restitution. Most of the statues and funeral monuments of the Upper Nile, like those of ancient Greece, were not stolen and do not fall within the Unesco protocol. They were legitimately removed not by stealth but by wealth, sometimes in league with politics. In time, politics will combine with wealth and restore them. If Londoners wish to gaze on Rameses II or Cleopatra's needle, if Parisians remain attached to the Luxor obelisk, they should gaze on a copy, as they now gaze on a copy of Michelangelo's *David*.

Most curators are averse to what they uncomfortably call 'de-acquisition'. Some fear for the integrity of their collections if left in the hands of possible mercenary trustees. Objects might be sold to pay running costs and relieve governments of the need for grants. That would clearly be wrong. But to pass from this reasonable concern to a refusal to discuss any restitution is intellectually feeble. Strict guidelines should be in place before any restitution could be considered. But to rule it out altogether is to open and keep open what will be a running sore. Somehow Britain must find a way to return the head of Rameses to the Nile and restore the caryatid maiden to Athens. If museum statutes are an obstacle, then statutes can be changed.

The heads of Europe's museums shudder at such talk. Where will it end? they cry. Better not let it begin. But 'it' has begun. Demands from countries of origin are certain to become more radical. The way to meet them is by pre-emption. Unesco might redeem its bruised reputation by drawing up a new convention, laying down a limited basis on which the return of legally acquired objects might take place. Museums must be reassured that all their possessions are not at risk. In my view, two categories only are appropriate for restitution.

The first is objects qualifying as 'crown jewels', artefacts located abroad that are seen as part of a country's identity, objects holding a collective symbolism for a nation and its people. This category might embrace the stone sarcophagi of the pharoahs, of which most tombs in the Valley of the Kings have been denuded and rendered meaningless. Egypt's equivalent of the tomb of Henry VII in Westminster Abbey is that of Seti I in the Valley of the Kings. Seti's beautifully inscribed sarcophagus lies forlorn on the ground floor of London's Soane Museum, seen by a tiny fraction of those who visit the Valley. The Elgin marbles also fall into this category, hard though it is for Britons to accept the eventual implication of this.

The second category is large monuments and architectural statuary taken from sites now open to the public: columns wrenched from Greek porticos, Egyptian colossi, Berlin's walls of Babylon. Such removals may have been legal and may have saved the objects at the time. But fragments of buildings should not be in museums when they can be back on the sites for which they were built. Many of these removals were regarded as vandalism when they occurred. Time does not make them less so. The British Museum or the Metropolitan in New York may gain professional kudos from displaying portions of Greek temples, but they offer no public benefit that could not be met by a replica.

Adequate conservation, pollution control and public display should be prerequisites for restitution. I believe the lists under my two categories would not be long – painful though they might be to prepare. No institution could argue that it is being stripped of its treasures. A wise museum would pre-empt any argument and negotiate possible exchanges of objects with museums in host countries. Indeed exchange without necessarily transferring formal ownership might be a way round some legal obstacles. There must be gaps in the British Museum's Egyptian department that could be filled from Cairo's voluminous vaults. So nervous are museum curators of this issue that few see the chance for improving their collections that restitution might offer.

Cultural diplomacy, the non-political intercourse between nations, is now expanding. From academic exchange to broadcasting to the arts to sport to tourism, the flow of people and ideas is creating new strains and new opportunities. This would put museums and galleries in the spotlight even without the nationalist and fundamentalist upsurges now being seen across Europe and the Middle East. The more people are on the move, voluntarily or as refugees, the more they will grasp at tangible memorials to their past. Ethnic studies are booming, as are ethnic conflicts. Where historic treasures have been taken from a people, they will fight to get them back, even at a cost to their political and commer-

120

cial interest. The Theban hills round Luxor were long haunted by the ghosts of foreign collectors crying, 'Mine, all mine'. Soon other ghosts will haunt the museums of the West. They will cry, 'Not yours but ours!', and go on crying until somebody listens.

15

IN A CITY CHURCHYARD

My CHURCHYARD lies far beneath my office window. Sunlight just penetrates its depths, sunk long ago beneath a plateau of City roofs. Its grass is green-black and tough as wire, roots buried in a rancid compost of leaves, soot and clay. Heaven only knows what that clay has seen. For a thousand years the soles of London feet have marched across it, as if to stamp its memories into oblivion. Round the perimeter stand the sentinels of the place, headstones of long-departed citizens laughably telling each other to rest in peace. Acid air has consumed their inscriptions and carried all memory of their owners to the winds. They are now meaningless obelisks. Overhead, squadrons of starlings and sparrows dispute the time of day with a scavenging pigeon. A lanky plane tree is their gymnasium, its bark scarred from a hundred years of City atmosphere. Leathery leaves allow little rain or sun to reach the grass below.

To one side is an old bench, dusted each lunchtime by anonymous backsides. Its chief beneficiaries are two old tramps for whom this churchyard is almost home. They know every grain and splinter. For all their daily stupor, they bear witness to the genius of the place, as I do from my window. Against the churchyard wall is a shed containing a broom, a spade and a weeding fork, emblems of office for that modern sexton, the Corporation gardener. The City fathers allow him an occasional geranium, gaudy rouge on an old black crone of a flowerbed.

The place of worship to which my churchyard owes allegiance has long departed, burnt to the ground in the Great Fire of 1666 and never rebuilt. But a church may come and go, a London churchyard is for ever. It is a place of enduring enchantment. No other city in the world has its equal. Churchyards are monuments to London's continuity. They are a visible link to its most distant past. Almost every central London churchyard predates the Reformation and some go back to the earliest Saxon settlements. They have survived in a legal limbo, protected by exclusion from acts of Parliament, consecrated, desecrated, hallowed and unhallowed but never quite disowned.

Even after the Great Fire, when 88 out of the City's 107 churches were destroyed, few dared touch the churchyards. A church is a building which can be deconsecrated, demolished and redeveloped. But God's acre is inhabited by departed citizens and defended by the law. Churches could be closed under the Union of Benefices Act. Churchyards were specifically outside its terms. To close a churchyard needs an individual act of Parliament. If you try, all the hobgoblins of Temple Lane – parish clerks, vestrymen, aldermen, canon lawyers in flowing gowns and wigs – will storm down Fleet Street and consume you in a hellfire of threats and fees. A dispute about a churchyard relegates Jarndyce and Jarndyce to summary justice. With primogeniture and Crown privilege, law on burial grounds is on the escutcheon of the British constitution, testament to our freedom from revolutionary upheaval. Despite the widespread redevelopment of the City since the war, only a dozen yards have been successfully closed.

London's churchyards are medieval not only in origin but also in shape. I know of none which is either a true square or a circle. Their borders owe nothing to the planner's set-square or the laws of geometry. They seem to have been hacked, pushed, sliced, squeezed, moulded between office block, church wall and pavement. But they have the whip hand. It is they that force property developers to sacrifice fortunes not just in land but in air space. To the architect or quantity surveyor, a churchyard is a natural hazard, a disaster. It must be faced as a navigator faces a magnetic storm, an act of God which defies all science. A few churchyards, notably in the more permissive West End, have been lifted bodily and dumped far away, like some old bag-lady who refuses to die. St James's, Piccadilly, pops up in Hampstead Road, St Martin-in-the-Fields in Pratt Street. But these are few. In the most expensive corner of the Square Mile, long-lost St Martin Outwich clings to its few square feet of garden. When in 1966 the bombed shell of St Mary, Aldermanbury, was taken down and rebuilt in Fulton, Missouri, the churchyard stayed behind to guard its shades.

Other English cities that had a large number of pre-Reformation churches, such as York and Norwich, have seen most of them disappear. London has been unique. The medieval City had 140 places of worship. It is astonishing that of these, over half survive today in some shape or form. And even where churches have gone, churchyards remain as compensation. As a result the historian Harvey Hackman (*London Churchyards*, Collins, 1981) has counted 73 yards still recognizable in the City and inner Westminster.

The story of these medieval relics is the story of London. They may once have been the sanctuaries of peace that many of their country cousins still are. Most were simply repositories for the urban dead, their corpses bursting from the confines of church vaults to fill every cubic foot of space on and below ground. The regular plagues of the sixteenth and seventeenth centuries saw corpses not so much buried as tossed into graveyards. During the Great Plague of 1665, lime was heaped on piles of bodies, raising the ground levels of many London churchyards by two or three feet – St Helen, Bishopsgate, for instance, or the melancholy yard of St Bartholomew the Great in Smithfield. Pepys recorded a visit to his local church of St Olave, Hart Street, in January 1666, 'It frighted me indeed to go through the church, more than I thought it could have done, to see so many graves lie so high upon the churchyard, where people have been buried of the plague. I was much troubled at it and do not think to go through it again a good while.'

By the early nineteenth century these graveyards were the epitome of urban desolation. Graves were dug over and over. Bodies were crammed on top of each other by families desperate to see loved ones interred in sacred soil. Corpses were stolen for dissec-

124

tion or merely shifted back and forth to make way for new arrivals. Many Londoners moved more often after their deaths than when still alive. What are now blessed oases in the urban desert were then the opposite, earthly manifestations of hell, a breeding ground of disease avoided by all but those whose poverty left them no option. Witnesses to a parliamentary select committee in 1842 testified that the mortality rate among families living adjacent to graveyards was three times higher than elsewhere in the same parish.

The rules governing paupers' graves stipulated that they had to be kept open until filled. Upwards of twenty bodies might be dumped in a pit until somebody thought to cover them with lime and soil. Hackman records a tragedy in the yard of St Botolph, Aldgate: in 1838 a gravedigger and a young fish-dealer who went to his assistance both died from the fumes arising from a paupers' grave into which the digger had descended. In 1842 a Dr G.A. Walker of Drury Lane led a campaign to reform graveyards and create new sites outside the city. He wrote of St Giles's churchyard south of Bloomsbury, 'Here in this place of Christian burial you may see human heads, covered with hair; here in this consecrated ground are human bones with flesh still adhering to them.' To Dickens they supplied some of his most graphic images of squalor. In *Sketches by Boz* he describes one as 'so pressed upon by houses, so small, so rank, so forgotten, except by the few people who ever look on them from their smokey windows. As I stand peeping in through the iron gates and rails, I can peel the rusty metal off, like bark from an old tree . . . one of my best loved I call the churchyard of St Ghastly Grim.' He reused this scene, apparently based on St Olave, Hart Street, in the terrible climax of *Bleak House*.

The tale of the reform of these sanctuaries is a microcosm of Victorian social improvement. Already in the early eighteenth century new churches, such as those promoted by Queen Anne, acquired burial sites away from their vicinity: St John, Smith Square, for instance, and St George, Bloomsbury. But it was not until 1832 that the first cemetery act was passed through Parliament for Kensal Green, a quarter-century after the foundation of Père Lachaise in Paris. There followed a flurry of burial acts in the 1850s enabling the cessation of burials in central London and the development of suburban cemeteries and crematoria, many of them architecturally ambitious and commercially profitable. Some never materialized, such as the vast mausoleum intended for Primrose Hill. Others are now historic memorials in their own right, Highgate, Nunhead, Brompton and Kensal, monuments to the 'Victorian way of death'. Their fantastic catacombs and chapels in coloured marble and granite, their tombstones and effigies, their motifs classical, Gothic, baroque and art nouveau, are as distant from our City churchyards as a New Town estate is from a smugglers' cove.

Some of the new burial grounds were linked to a mother church in the City or Westminster, others were purely commercial. In departing the city centre they took with them the ceremony and sense of purpose that had attached to the environs of the old churches. In no sense were they any longer the town equivalent of that peculiar English institution, the country churchyard. The City yards now saw a mercifully brief period of upheaval. In the mid-Victorian period when acts of Parliament were relatively easy to obtain, many were sold or merged into surrounding properties. Not until 1884 was a Disused Burial Grounds Act passed, specifically outlawing the use of graveyards for building purposes other than by the Church itself. This accompanied the founding of the Metropolitan Public Gardens Association, committed to converting former and existing churchyards into gardens. These were eventually maintained by local councils. This municipalization of the churchyards was inevitable if they were to survive and continue to be tended. Yet it is ironic that of the large inner city burial grounds, the one that is most evocative today, the Nonconformist Bunhill Fields north of the Barbican, was never attached to a particular place of worship. Its magnificent Georgian chest tombs and crowded memorials give some impression of what an ancient City churchyard must have been like before population growth burst its boundaries. Founded in the seventeenth century, first for plague victims and then for Dissenters, Bunhill swallowed an astonishing 120,000 bodies before its closure in 1853.

The churchyards survived, as public gardens, pocket parks or meagre open spaces. Some became little more than grass verges to a widened road, such as All Hallows, London Wall. The Victorians transformed them from religious sanctuaries to symbols of civic pride. They were tidied and replanted. Headstones were studied, their inscriptions copied (by the assiduous Percy Rushden, who in 1910 published his *Churchyard Inscriptions of the City of London*). Seats were placed along footpaths, designed and redesigned to discourage tramps from using them as beds. Paths were coated with asphalt, rarely with the York stone traditional for London pavements. Robust exotics from Kew were set in tasteful boxes to do battle with London's fumes.

For all this care and attention City churchyards have never totally surrendered to municipalization. Those who look on them as mere amenities miss their point and miss much of their atmosphere. For amenity we can seek out the open prairies of the Royal Parks or the genteel avenues and squares of West London. City churchyards are for connoisseurs of urban struggle, of the battle between past and present, between nature and the more offensive works of man. They have been fighting, most of them, for seven or eight centuries. Their rolls of honour are carved on the plaques, memorials and gravestones: 'The parish names cut deep and strong/ To hold the shades of evening long,' wrote John Betjeman.

Each churchyard mounts its idiosyncratic defence against the city's assault. That of St Clement Danes rises like a bow wave round Wren's sturdy galleon as it braves the winds of verbiage that once poured out of Fleet Street. The statue of Dr Johnson stands bold on its prow. The churchyard of St Mary-at-Hill is like a castle dungeon, so grim that even the ghosts must shudder and flee at nightfall. At St Andrew, Holborn, a burst of civic horticulture rises over the battlements as if the flora itself were an outer bailey. Giant planes guard the crippled corpse of St Anne, Soho, while the churchyard of the actors' church, St Paul, Covent Garden, has withdrawn altogether, tortoise-like behind its walls and iron railings. Anyone who can find Dickens's secluded churchyard of St Peter, Cornhill, deserves an award. It is down a private alley, where 'conveniently and healthfully elevated above the level of the living were the dead and the tombstones, some of the latter droopingly inclined from the perpendicular as if ashamed of the lies they told' (*Our Mutual Friend*).

Nobody would have proposed or planned these places. They will not be found in any urban design manual or in any new city. They are unintended, unobtrusive polygons of natural sound, of leaves rustling, of birds chattering, of humans murmuring to each other above the cacophony of mechanical combustion. They are havens in which company executives, secretaries and clerks can all ride out the storms of City business. Here office workers find relief from tedium, labourers relax on cool grass and children escape from nagging discipline.

My London office looked down on the churchyard of St Anne, Blackfriars. Its abbey once stood by the mouth of the old Fleet ditch but long ago vanished. The abbey nave was then given over as churchyard to the adjacent St Anne's, but now that also has vanished. Its churchyard alone survives, a forgotten pool among the cliffs south of Carter Lane. Into that pool I used to toss my dreams, as thousands of City workers must have done before. I would stir them in among the stones, nourish them in summer with a few rays of sunlight. At night, when I was last in the office and the lights were out, these dreams would come to life and dance with the spirits of Londoners departed, whirling back and forth down the seven ages of the City. The night wanted only the magic lamplighter and his wand. In such places the past becomes our present and we transcend ourselves.

16

HAMPSTEAD'S
SECRET ARTISTS

To one who has been long in city pent,
'Tis very sweet to look into the fair
And open face of heaven.

KEATS'S LINES on Hampstead well express the quality that has
always drawn Londoners to this leafy hillside, the quality of
escape. Since the seventeenth century it has been a retreat from
the noise and dirt of the metropolis, within the city's reach yet
with some of the aura of a country town. Hampstead is London's
Montmartre, its Georgetown, its Grinzing, yet it is more distinctive
than all these. Hampstead is height, air, health – and thus for most
of its history, wealth. For a few it has been a source of artistic
inspiration. The town's qualification as an artists' colony is tenu-
ous. But Hampstead artists there have been, some famous and
some neglected. The latter are the more intriguing chroniclers.

The natural features of Hampstead Heath – the clarity of its
light and its views towards London – long recommended it to
painters of the English landscape school. Richard Wilson was an
early visitor. George Romney built himself a house on Holly Hill
in 1796, 'freed from town distractions . . . to paint pictures of
exalted purpose and imaginative force', anything but the miserable
portraits from which he regretted having to eke a living. Copley

Fielding lived briefly at Capo di Monte. In the 1820s John Linnell and William Collins rented Wyldes Farm at North End. William Blake, John Varley, George Morland and Samuel Palmer visited them there. They strode across the Heath and communed with the spirits of the place. But of these only Linnell left many paintings inspired by Hampstead itself.

The Royal Academician Clarkson Stanfield moved to what was already known as 'the town' in 1847 and was for many years doyen of its cultural life. Ford Madox Brown, after a brief visit, spent eleven years painting his much-reproduced study of *Work*, based on a Heath Street scene he had witnessed from his studio window. The most distinguished Hampstead artist was John Constable. He wrote to his friend Archdeacon Fisher of the family's new house in Well Walk, 'Our little drawing room commands a view unsurpassed in Europe, from Westminster Abbey to Gravesend. The dome of St Paul's in the air seems to realize Michelangelo's words on seeing the Pantheon: I will build such a thing in the sky.' Constable arrived first in 1819 and returned regularly for the rest of his life, 'to hear the trees and the clouds ask me to do something like them'. In 1820 he moved his family to Hampstead and produced the first of his studies of climate and clouds, most of them executed in the vicinity of Whitestone Pond. He left dozens of paintings, watercolours and notebook sketches as testament to his enthusiasm. Constable and his family are buried in the parish churchyard of St John's in Church Row.

Labouring in the shadow of these well-known names was a different group of artists, the producers of topographical prints. These are the forgotten footsoldiers of local history. Their work was often uncatalogued. Usually their identities can be summoned from the archives only by deciphering a scratched signature or monogram at the foot of an etching plate. Yet from the start of the Georgian era to the advent of photography, these artists were the most astute witnesses of the city's changing appearance. Their silent evidence brings old maps to life and clothes old buildings in history. Together with their equally neglected cousins, the watercolourists, they are indispensable to any historian of London topography.

Most printmakers worked in Hampstead simply to satisfy a demand. They drew and they etched because the public wanted pictures of the town and countryside round London. The market for topographical prints emerged in the course of the eighteenth century, mostly through the enterprise of the engraver-turned-publisher John Boydell. This market was further exploited by Boydell's chief competitor, Rudolph Ackermann, a German immigrant who had premises in the Strand from 1795. It reached its zenith in the fashion, indeed the passion, for 'picturesque' prints of old buildings and nature which flourished under the Regency.

Hampstead was the nearest place to London that could reasonably claim the epithet of picturesque. The village featured in most best-sellers of Regency topography, in Britton and Brayley's *Beauties of England and Wales* (1801–18) and in Westall and Finden's *Great Britain Illustrated* (1830). It was portrayed as a cottagey settlement buried in lush woodland. The Heath was shown as enjoying scenery worthy of the Lake District. To the south the railway artist John Bourne showed the new Primrose Hill tunnel as a Piranesian dungeon. But two artists of the period claim special attention both by the volume of their output and by their special commitment to Hampstead, Captain Thomas Hastings and George Childs. Their prints have been admirably researched by Jonathan Ditchburn.

Captain Hastings was a sailor, a collector of customs and amateur etcher. His work was limited in scope and also in quality. He copied some paintings of Richard Wilson, for whom he had a great admiration, and published a set of etchings of Canterbury under the title *Vestiges of Antiquity*. We can imagine him as the sort of cultivated public servant already emerging as a resident of suburban London. His etchings of Hampstead appeared between 1822 and 1831, but they constitute the limit of our knowledge of him. Hastings's Heath is unlike that of any other artist, spare of trees, its contours gashed and savaged for quarrying sand. Strange Lowry-esque people seem to wander lost amid an undulating sea of hillocks. Hastings's view along Spaniards Road, before this part of the Heath was excavated, might be a route across a bare Castilian plain. His etchings are almost surreal in their emptiness, their love of sky. He was truly a sailor artist.

George Childs could not have been more different. While

Hastings worked with the hard, economical line of the etching needle, Childs employed the softer, more luxuriant tones of lithography, using chalk on stone to produce a picture for impression. He was active in the 1840s, perhaps a time when the Heath was less abused by quarrying and when vegetation had begun to cover some of its worse scars. Childs loved trees. He published a volume entitled *English Landscape Scenery and Woodland Sketches* and another, containing twenty-four magnificent Hampstead scenes, called *Childs' Advanced Drawing Book*. The only extant copy of this book is at the Yale Center for British Art in America. The prints, almost all of them recognizably of locations in and around the Heath, are admirable examples of the romantic revival. They show local people going about their daily affairs in quiet harmony with nature. Over their heads is always a protective canopy of Childs' beloved trees.

To browse through the work of these artists is to be intrigued by how they lived and worked. We know nothing of them but the pictures. They were probably comfortable amateurs, residents of a town already attracting wealthy 'second homers' for weekend and summer retreats. I am sure they would be surprised and delighted that future historians should comb their plates for evidence of a lost building here or a clump of trees there.

No such pleasure came the way of a third artist, David Lucas, mezzotinter to John Constable. If the Hampstead of Hastings was desolate and of Childs sylvan, that of Lucas was tormented. His task was to reproduce in mezzotint the tempestuous clouds and storms first captured by Constable in oil or watercolour. Constable had been much taken by the success of Turner's landscape mezzotints. His intention was to emulate them not for money but, so he initially claimed, to promote the study of the rural scenery of England 'with her climate of more than vernal freshness, in whose summer skies and rich autumnal clouds the observer of nature may daily watch her endless varieties of effect'.

To Constable such an effect bordered on obsession. 'The sky is the source of light in nature, and governs everything,' he wrote. His Hampstead sky sketches were revolutionary expressions of the new science of climatology. The impact on his art is well described by Olive Cook in her essay on Constable's Hampstead:

The transient play of light on clouds, foliage, chimney pots and sun-warmed walls has never been so precisely recorded in pigment as in these sketches. The subtle changes wrought in the colour and movement of the sky by shifting winds at different times of the day and season have never been more surely transfixed by so penetrating an eye. Yet this eye, quick and faithful as the camera's lens, was that of a poet not a machine, emotion as well as accurate observation guides the charged brush. The impact of the resulting images of torn November skies coldly reflected in chill water, of the burst of the westering sun through a thicket, of pigeons tumbling against purple rain clouds, of a sky so sultry that we almost feel the oily drops that splashed down onto Constable's palette, can be likened only to those rare moments of enhanced sensibility when we find ourselves at one with the universe.

What was Lucas to make of that? To reproduce such an effect on metal rather than in a sketchbook or on a canvas gave him unending trouble. Mezzotint involves roughening a copper plate with a rocker and then smoothing the parts required to print light or white. The technique produces intense tonal contrast, with darkness a velvety black. It was much favoured by portraitists to reproduce their work but less so by conventional landscape artists. Outlines tended to become imprecise and patches of dark were particularly gloomy – an impressionistic effect that appealed to Turner and Constable. Mezzotint required of the engraver skills as exacting as those of the original artist. He was not reproducing a line, but recreating a response to landscape and, in Constable's case, a response to skyscape.

Lucas's copies of Constable's Hampstead pictures are mostly of the upper Heath. They are stormy, dark pictures full of menace. Rain is coming up over Harrow, dark deeds are threatened on Haverstock Hill, a crouched sand digger is about to be hit by lightning or dazzled by a rainbow. Not surprisingly, Constable complained that Lucas's impression of these scenes was not exactly the same as his. Their correspondence is littered with abuse. One plate, sent back in an early state, 'looks as if all the chimney sweepers in Christendom have been at work on it and thrown their soot bags up in the air . . . the sky is and always will be rotten'. Rembrandt had no soot bag, cried Constable. Lucas might have replied that Rembrandt did not work in mezzotint, and usually did his own engraving. The relationship was not a happy one. Constable came to view the entire enterprise with dismay: 'All my reflections on the subject go to oppress me, its duration, its expense, its impossibility of remuneration.'

Constable's career recovered from what he saw as a failure. Lucas's did not. He had hitched his wagon to Constable's star and had been unhitched. He disappeared into drunkenness and poverty. Yet I find Lucas's prints 'after Constable' superb landscapes, works of art in their own right. On occasion, Constable did recognize this. He was one of the few artists of his period to acknowledge that painter and printmaker were engaged in a joint creative endeavour. He even wrote of Lucas's 'beautiful feeling and execution' and of the 'lovely amalgamation of our works'. Andrew Shirley, in his study of Constable's mezzotints, wrote that Lucas's work achieved 'a richness and depth of tone rarely surpassed' in this exacting medium. But Lucas was to reappear only in 1881, when he is recorded as dying in a Fulham workhouse. Like so many printmakers he was left to nurse an unrecognized talent that when far beyond craftsmanship.

Of all Hampstead artists, the most elusive but potentially engaging is a Frenchman who visited the area in the early Georgian period. He coincided with the revival in the Hampstead Wells's fashionability in the 1740s. The Hampstead of Jean Baptiste Chatelain was much changed from the frenetic and vulgar day-trip resort of the 1720s. Public assemblies were still held in Well Road, but the notorious Long Room had become a chapel and local doctors and publicans were forced to ever more desperate measures to sustain the popularity of the chalybeate spring, from which the Wells had derived its original appeal. In 1734 a Dr John Soames wrote a book claiming that the British race was in a state of advanced degeneration. The cause was its consumption of vast quantities of tea. Chalybeate, dancing, riding and smoking were the only antidotes. Hampstead, according to the wisdom of the day, had to avoid any return to plebeian entertainment. It had to move 'up market' to attract prosperous, presumably hypochondriac customers. Chatelain's prints were directed to that end.

Where Hastings found inspiration in Richard Wilson and Lucas in John Constable, Chatelain paid his allegiance to his countryman, Gaspar Poussin. His *Prospects of Hampstead and Highgate* appeared in 1750 and 1752, priced at five shillings a set. The debt to Poussin is evident, indeed blatant. Hampstead is portrayed as an arcadian landscape of the utmost gentility. Fashionably dressed visitors promenade across fields and down lanes filled with happy shepherds and well-fed animals. The world is at peace in a Chatelain print. The working classes are strictly pastoral. According to the historian Samuel Redgrave, Chatelain was a relaxed artist. He produced his prints for the ubiquitous John Boydell and 'worked only when impelled by necessity. It was his custom to hire himself by the hour, working as long as the fit lasted and bargaining for instant payment.' As to why he swiftly vanished as a topographical artist, Redgrave was in no doubt: 'His great talents were obscured by his depraved manners and irregularities.' He died like Lucas in poverty but at least in a fashion true to his ancestry, as a result of eating a huge meal.

These artists were the last to picture Hampstead as a community separate from the metropolis. This separation ended in the mid-nineteenth century with the outward push of the city. George Cruikshank's famous satirical print, *The March of Bricks of Mortar* of 1829, was occasioned by the building of Finchley Road. That thoroughfare brought with it new cohorts of builders, who were to lay siege to the northern slopes. By the middle of the century, wave upon wave of brick and stucco assailed Hampstead from all quarters, from Belsize, from Camden, from South End. Fitzjohn's Avenue was fired across the fields to smash into the end of Heath Street. By then, the printmakers were turning from country to town. Their task now was to celebrate the religious and municipal institutions of a booming community. They soon abandoned etching and lithography for the easier and cruder medium of the woodcut, more suitable for mass reproduction. Their principal outlet was the *Illustrated London News*.

If the objective of Hampstead artists was no longer to show the picturesque qualities of the Heath, one reason was that it had been partly supplanted in popularity by more distant beauties accessible by railway. In addition, the Heath was no longer under threat. The Victorian campaign to save the Heath, one of the longest and fiercest of all conservation battles, not only secured for Hampstead and for London a great amenity. It also preserved the scenery recorded by local artists over the previous century. The Heath is now a landscape frozen in time. To a remarkable extent, the Hampstead of Chatelain and Hastings, Childs and Lucas is the Hampstead of today.

17

THE VALE OF HEALTH

CHARLES DICKENS enjoyed satirizing London's local historians. He opened *Pickwick Papers* with its hero speculating pedantically 'On the Source of Hampstead Ponds'. The Pickwick Club was assembled to witness the 'gigantic brain' of its founder as he traced those mighty waterways to their source. The Amazon and the Nile held no greater challenge. Dickens did not reveal the outcome of Mr Pickwick's speculation, presumably stimulated by Dickens's own residence in Hampstead's North End. But those of Pickwickian curiosity could do worse than start, and perhaps end, their search in the marshy purlieus of the Vale of Health.

To my mind there is no odder place in London, or one with a more curious history. The villages that once sat on the outer rim of Hampstead – North End, South End, West End – were always its colonies. Not so the Vale of Health. Its three lanes and an alley entirely surrounded by Heath lie in a thickly wooded dell, approached by a single track. It is nobody's colony. It is an independent state, London's San Marino or Andorra. It should print its own stamps and have cross-gartered gendarmes.

Early references to the site are as a malarial swamp, thus plausibly one source of the famous ponds. It was directly below the squatted community of Littleworth on the Heath summit near what is now Jack Straw's Castle. In the late eighteenth century land in

137

this neighbourhood was owned by Samuel Hatch, and the low-lying marsh was known as Hatches Bottom. The then holders of Littleworth property decided to move poorer residents from their cottages and sell what was prime building land for development. The removals coincided with the draining of Hatches Bottom in 1777 for a new Hampstead reservoir. The evicted residents were housed in a row of cottages described as poor houses just above the reservoir.

The paupers remained isolated on the Heath. The site was tainted by its past as a swamp and by its status as a home for displaced persons. A desire to wipe out these associations is the most obvious reason for the change of name from Hatches Bottom to Vale of Health, a change first recorded in 1801. (Another explanation is that somebody misspelled the word Heath.) Hence a new Hampstead settlement had been established and new arrivals came to exploit what was potentially an attractive location. The paupers soon found themselves displaced yet again. Residents annexed Heath waste for their gardens, and eventually for new building.

Prints of the Vale in the early 1800s show the small cottages with gardens marked by a stockade to keep out the cattle. The only distinctive feature of these pictures is St Paul's, floating on the distant horizon. Yet within ten years the Vale was considered desirable enough to be occupied by middle-class residents, one of whom lent his house in 1815 to his son-in-law, Leigh Hunt, the poet and essayist. Hunt was recently released from prison, incarcerated for libelling the 50-year-old Prince Regent as 'a violater of his word, a libertine over head and ears in disgrace, and a despiser of domestic ties'. He had earlier lived on the other side of the Heath and now returned eagerly to the same district. 'No rhapsodist ever loved a mountain solitude . . . more than Hunt loved that place,' wrote his biographer, Edmund Blunden. He wrote sonnets in its honour, some of purple phraseology, describing 'cottaged vales with pillowy fields beyond/ And clump of darkening pines and prospects blue.'

Hunt stayed in the Vale from 1815 to 1819 and again in 1821, before visiting Shelley in Italy, a visit that coincided with the latter's death. His hospitality in Hampstead to Keats, Shelley, Lamb, Hazlitt and other radical writers of the time brought the Vale much glory. In 1816 Keats wrote after a visit that he was 'brimful of the friendliness/ That in a little cottage I have found.' Another visitor, Horace Smith, describes musical and literary evenings round the fireside: 'Shelley with the blue eyes, the stooping tallness, the earnest unmusical voice; Keats shy, embarrassed as unused to society, speaking little.' All would tramp across the Heath to the small enclosure and exchange fulsome compliments on each other's work. The sociability became increasingly fey. Sonnet competitions were held. Hunt would crown Keats with laurel sprigs. Keats would crown Hunt with ivy.

An unofficial plaque declares that all this took place in a cottage on the site of the present South Villa, next to what has confusingly been named Hunt Cottage. This attribution appears to rest on a local postman's recollection in the 1890s. Helen Bentwich, in her exhaustive history of the Vale, debates the matter at a length that would do credit to Mr Pickwick. She points out that Hunt at the time had a large family, a servant, a study and a piano, not to mention the considerable dining table now in Keats House off Downshire Hill. He was clearly able to entertain in style, and in his garden in summer. No Vale property was entered in the rate books under Hunt's name, but appears to have been acquired and lent to him by his wife's father, presumably a gentleman of means. This suggests a more substantial property than one of the tiny cottages. In 1865 the *Art Journal* firmly credited the larger Vale Lodge as Hunt's residence. Edmund Blunden in his life of Leigh Hunt puts him in the second largest, Pavilion Cottage, now Manor Lodge. This property was once lived in by Helen, Lady Dufferin, and was mentioned in 1848 as possessing 'garden, conservatory, coach-house and stable'. Nobody seems to know for sure.

This debate at least shows that by the Regency period the Vale had changed from pauper settlement to acceptable address for a gentleman. The middle years of the nineteenth century saw both a sudden expansion in the Vale's population and a further change in character. In 1855, a developer named Donald Nicoll purchased the original paupers' cottages from the Poor Law Guardians. On the site he erected a row of small houses and in 1863 a hotel. All had gardens running down to the edge of the reservoir, which Nicoll graced with the title of lake. The following year a lithograph advertisement was published showing a large building opened by the 'Suburban Hotel Company' with the aim of attracting visitors up the hill from the new Hampstead Junction railway station at South End. A second hotel was soon opened almost next door, for some reason designed to look like a chapel. The first hotel became the Vale of Health Tavern and offered day-trippers a tea garden, assembly rooms, terraces, grottoes and boating on the lake. Boasting accommodation for 2,000, it enjoyed immense, if short-lived, commercial success, reviving the eighteenth-century appeal of Hampstead to the London proletariat.

Hampstead, with the exception of the poor enclave round New End, was an almost exclusively middle-class suburb. Censuses showed it with the lowest percentage of impoverished and one of the highest numbers of servants per head of any London parish. The reaction of local residents to Nicoll's venture in the Vale was as hostile as it would doubtless be today. In 1863, the poet James Thomson wrote caustically, 'Babble and gabble you rabble,/ A thousand in full yell,/ And this is your tower of Babel,/ This not-to-be-finished hotel.' Yet the hotel was finished and flourished for at least a decade. It would have received a fillip with the advent of Bank Holidays in 1871 which greatly increased the popularity of the Heath. Train-borne trippers poured out of Hampstead Station and made their way to the summit, the path taking them directly through the Vale. Prints of the time show the Heath as a packed landscape of holidaymakers, gypsies, pickpockets and footpads. Bentwich cites one resident of the Vale who was 'obliged to draw down my blinds from twelve until dark on Bank Holidays' such were the obscenities on view beyond.

The present Vale is the one that Nicoll created. The community had just fourteen houses at the start of his investment. By 1880 it had thirty-two houses and by 1890 fifty-three. From what I can detect, only two modern buildings have been erected since and both on previously built-up sites. The total enclosed area is just six acres. When he had exhausted his market, Nicoll expended much effort in preventing anybody else building nearby. He became a prominent figure in the Heath preservation lobby, his arch-enemy being the lord of the manor, Maryon Wilson, who wished to lay out housing estates across much of the East Heath.

Wilson even built a bridge over one of the ponds in preparation for his main road; it stands today as an incongruous folly in one of the wildest corners of the Heath. Nicoll chaired public meetings and raised petitions to Parliament citing the 'loss of public amenity' that would result from further building. Hypocrite he may have been. He was at least successful in helping to forestall others like him.

What Nicoll does not appear to have achieved is the ambition of every London property developer, a stable middle-class enclave. His houses were by Hampstead standards small. The frontages were mean and the gardens narrow strips of land. Combined with the garishness of the two hotels, the Vale appears by the 1880s to have taken on a character very different from the rest of Hampstead. In 1882 the Salvation Army marked out its degenerate habits by selecting it for its Hampstead headquarters. It marched on the Vale and, amid 'desperate fighting', pitched camp in part of the second hotel. At the time this was improbably called the Athenaeum and was a drinking and dancing club popular with London's German community. Bentwich has a report of the Salvationists' meeting 'with a Hallelujah Free-and-Easy, wound up with some short sharp firing and Heaven-commanding power; one man came out with a tremble and fell into the fountain'. Battles between the Army and the Vale's drinking population were a much-deplored feature of Hampstead life. Sundays reverberated to the sound of shouts, trumpets and drums. The German club survived until the Great War.

Many London communities have undergone wide fluctuations in their social character, usually related to the age and size of their properties and the stages of building cycles. Yet of this we know little. I am surprised at how little research is done into the occupancy of individual London houses and streets, and thus into the local dynamics of London's economy. A single house in Canonbury or Campden Hill, in Stockwell or Chalk Farm may have been lived in by a banker or a bricklayer at different stages in its history. It may have had a single family with servants or half a dozen families of labourers. It may have been the pride and joy of an ambitious entrepreneur or merely an overnight speculation by a local builder. The only certainty is that every property is always at the mercy of market forces and that these forces can drastically alter the character of a neighbourhood.

Donald Nicoll was plainly the dominant character in the Vale's history. In the words of Hampstead's most recent historian, F.M.L. Thompson, he succeeded however unintentionally in 'converting the Vale of Health from a few peaceful cottages into a raucous mini-town with gin-palace-style hotel and vulgar amusement gardens'. No other part of Hampstead experienced this upheaval. Yet by the turn of the century, the Vale appears to have recovered its earlier tranquillity. The hotel, damned by the Salvationists as 'the devil's barracks', was converted into artists' studios (one of them occupied by Stanley Spencer). It was finally demolished for flats in 1964. The Athenaeum too has been replaced by flats. By then the Vale had recovered its poise and merged into the social mileu of the rest of Hampstead, its residents mostly prosperous and its house prices high.

The only memorial to the Vale of the Nicoll period is the strange, scruffy fair that he installed on waste ground next to the hotel. Despite its appearance of a gypsy encampment, or perhaps because of it, the fairground has survived unaffected by the gentrification of the area. The right of tenure enjoyed by the Gray family, sometime owners of the hotel, has continued throughout this century. The fair is intermittently active at weekends, sometimes offering a roundabout, sometimes offering donkey rides on the Heath. But on spring and autumn Bank Holidays the ghosts of the past return in earnest. The site immediately above the Vale is taken over by a large modern funfair. The neighbourhood briefly reverts to its former, vulgar self. Revellers stream up the hill from South End. Youths gather in the shadows, frightening residents, dancing and yelling in the alleyways. This was once their place and they mean to haunt it for ever.

18

HUNTING THE GUITARIST

I FIRST laid eyes on Vermeer's *Guitar Player* in 1974 when she was convalescing on her stretcher in a humble workroom. She had been stolen from Kenwood House and discovered three months later in the churchyard of St Bartholomew's, Smithfield. I wondered if hers had been a willing elopement. Had she finally slipped from her frame one night and dashed through the woods of Hampstead towards the distant lights of London? Why had her abductor despaired of his prize? Having gone to all that trouble, what misery had overwhelmed him? And why abandon his captive in that bleak churchyard in Smithfield?

She is now back in a more secure captivity, imprisoned on her cold North London hilltop, plucking her guitar and gazing softly into the unknown. For companionship, she has only the elderly Rembrandt, a stern chaperone by Ferdinand Bol, a Frans Hals cavalier and, as the most likely auditor for her song, Van Dyck's dashing young Duke of Richmond. But she retreats even from them. She is barely visible. The glass behind which she is enclosed for further protection reflects a bleak room and the trees of Kenwood swaying outside. She seems utterly alone. There is no more poignant young lady in London.

Who was she? Indeed was she anybody in particular? *The Guitar Player* has fascinated me ever since that first meeting. The painting is one of London's masterpieces yet also one of its most neglected. Vermeer scholarship has paid it little attention. Yet I long to know

143

all there is to know about a picture. In the case of a portrait, my understanding and enjoyment are enhanced by knowing who is the sitter. My response is bound to differ if I am told that it is a commercial model or an imagined figure or a friend or loved one of the artist. Can we know this of *The Guitar Player*, untitled and unsigned as it is? Can we make so much as an educated guess?

I believe we can at least discover a little more than nothing, aided by the recent archival researches of the new Hercule Poirot of Vermeer studies, the American John Montias. A bibliography of some 200 works has been devoted to analysing Vermeer's few paintings and constructing something approaching a personality behind them. Yet this effort seems to me only to have opened up an ever greater distance between us and him. Vermeer resides in a category of his own among Dutch masters, one of an enticing elusiveness. Since so little can be said of him for sure, speculation has enjoyed a free rein. His work has been laden with metaphysical import. Conjecture has piled on conjecture. No artist has suffered more from obscurantism. Even the Dutch Vermeer scholar P.T.A. Swillens pleads with us 'not to begin by placing Vermeer on a pedestal as a philosopher, or as one inspired, or as a genius'. I want to bring him a little closer to the earth. I want to search what is known of Vermeer's life and family for any clues to the identity of his models and of this young woman in particular. The result is bound to be conjecture.

The Guitar Player, like all but two of Vermeer's pictures, is undated but is believed to have been executed in about 1671. Evidence for such dating is highly speculative, based largely on the picture's style. Since Vermeer was said by his wife to have ceased painting in 1672 – he died in December 1675 – it must therefore be among his last works. He would have been 38 or 39 at the time and on the brink of the collapse in his fortunes which came with the outbreak of the French war in 1672, Holland's Year of Calamity. For the next four years he struggled to rescue his affairs and borrow money to support Catharina, his wife, and their eleven children. He died in debt when just 43 and Catharina was forced to sue for bankruptcy. Her sad inventory of his belongings is one of the few records that exist of her husband's life.

There can be no such thing as a biography of Vermeer, only

a collecting of disparate fragments. His apparent conversion to Catholicism to marry his wife, Catharina Bolnes, in 1653 wiped him from parish records and from formal contact with his own family. It also prevented him from holding civic office. Little has been discovered of his family or friends, despite Montias's efforts in combing Dutch notarial archives for every reference to them. Of his professional life, we know only that he was elected a member of the Delft painters' guild at the time of his marriage and was twice elected a guild headman. Delft was a town with an active artistic life of which we have many records, yet the name of Johannes Vermeer occurs barely six times in them.

Montias, who believes he has found for Vermeer a patron in Pieter van Ruijven, admits there is no evidence beyond Vermeer being a beneficiary in the latter's will. Some twenty Vermeers were mentioned in van Ruijven's estate, though not until some time after Vermeer's death. Few pictures by Vermeer are mentioned in sales during his life. Nor are we sure how much of his total output (possibly of forty pictures) was still in his house on his death. He may have sold a couple a year. He may have sold hardly any. A French visitor asking for one in 1663 was sent away empty-handed, but did find a Vermeer at the house of a wealthy local baker. It is at least conceivable – and is my belief – that Vermeer painted chiefly for his personal pleasure and sold few of his works, perhaps to van Ruijven or to close friends. What is unlikely is that he painted and sold far more pictures than we know of today. We are certainly facing an unconventional Dutch painter.

Vermeer was a member of the guild and must therefore have been apprenticed. We do not know to whom. A much-vaunted influence was Carel Fabritius, three of whose pictures Vermeer at one time owned. But he died in 1654 when Vermeer was just 22. Vermeer is known to have acquired works by the Caravaggio enthusiast, Baburen of Utrecht. He traded in Italian masters, imitated them in his earliest period and used them in his compositions. Certainly there was no school of Vermeer, no 'studio' of Vermeer, no known pupils of Vermeer. He does not appear to have taught others. He appears briefly to have known Ter Borch and must have met de Hooch during the latter's short stay in Delft. On Fabritius's premature death, the young Vermeer was once mentioned in terms that implied an acknowledged talent. He certainly called himself a painter. But he emerges from this historical fog not as a professional artist in the manner of Metsu or Ter Borch, more a secluded family man, fascinated by the techniques of painting rather than by any commercial potential.

How many Vermeers exist? is a favourite party question. At the latest count, only thirty-two pictures are universally accepted as by him, with a further four as probably so. After decades of combing sales records and comparing Vermeer with other artists of the period, scholars doubt whether there were more than twenty lost works, and probably less. For a Dutch artist of the period, this is a small output. Nor did Vermeer leave drawings, notebooks, letters or other background material to his work. He executed no portraits of distinguished citizens or groups. He portrayed little of the vitality of mid-seventeenth century Holland, the informality of de Hooch, the society glamour of Metsu and Ter Borch or the boisterousness of Jan Steen and van Ostade. Vermeer's context was his home, the medium-sized Delft house belonging to his mother-in-law, Maria Thins, furnished with carpets, pictures, books and musical instruments. There is not a dimension of that house on Oude Langendijck that has not been reconstructed and refurnished (on the basis of his wife's inventory). Every window frame, chair back, inscription, floortile and droplet of light has been analysed. The emblem books have been studied and hidden messages sought. Yet his personality and the identity of his subjects remain obscure.

Vermeer's treatment of his human models adds further layers of obscurity. He seems to bring down a veil between viewer and subject. He pushes his scenes away behind lush curtains, through doorways, across tables. In only six pictures is there not an obvious space between artist and model. Vermeer's use of a camera obscura has been much debated. This was a lens reflecting an image on to a mirror and then on to a screen or even a canvas, and was popular in Holland at the time. The camera distanced the artist from the subject and focused attention on a single plane, as if seeing a subject in two dimensions. The lens could be adjusted or ground in such a way as to fracture the play of light on the screen: some students have even recreated Vermeer's 'impressionist' effect by means of such a lens. This is taken as explaining Vermeer's characteristic droplets of whites and yellows and his often out-of-focus foregrounds and backgrounds.

The elusiveness of the man and the paucity of his work left Vermeer long neglected. In the 1830s a connoisseur, John Smith, declared him to be an imitator of de Hooch but was baffled by his small output. He wrote, 'It is quite inexplicable how he attained the excellence many of [his works] exhibit.' The French critic Théophile Thore, who first catalogued and promoted Vermeer in the mid-nineteenth century, referred to him as his 'sphinx'. He was admired by the Impressionists. His pointillist technique was compared to Seurat. Similarities can be found with Matisse. Vermeer's most effusive modern admirer, Lawrence Gowing, portrayed him as a man apart: 'Vermeer is drawn away from his time to express the subtlest and least expressible meanings of humanity.' Gowing invested his subject with intense metaphysical import. 'He seems almost not to care, or not even to know, what it is that he is painting. What do men call this wedge of light? A nose? A finger? What do we know of its shape? To Vermeer none of this matters, the conceptual world of names and knowledge is forgotten, nothing concerns him but what is visible.'

Others have emphasized Vermeer's aloofness, his ethereal calm, his obsession with light to the exclusion of feeling. Marcel Proust has Bergotte confronting the *View of Delft* and seeing his own life 'in one pan of a heavenly scales, while the other contained the little patch of wall so finely painted in yellow'. To Proust, Vermeer's work was 'marked by withdrawal and silence . . . Passion, suffering and sex were banished from his art.' Critic after critic has knelt before this 'bird of paradise in the farmyard of Dutch painting' and concluded that only the most cerebral of geniuses can have been at work. So rarely did the muse of seventeenth-century Holland visit this house in Delft that she must have conveyed some special inspiration.

Vermeer can scarcely have made much money from his pictures, least of all to support his large family. There were two more likely sources of income. His wife declared after his death that he was an art dealer, he bought and sold paintings. This was at times a regular and potentially lucrative business in seventeenth-century

Holland. Every burgher's house was filled with paintings. Even servants' quarters were adorned with them. Dutch painters were seen as craftsmen, decorators, storytellers and moralists as well as interpreters of the classical Italian masters. Pictures by well-known artists not only fetched high prices but, like tulip bulbs, could experience wide speculative fluctuations. The career of an art dealer would have been both profitable and risky.

The inventory of Vermeer's possessions on his death included a large stock of paintings which, his wife explained, could not be sold because of the severity of the post-1672 recession. We have no knowledge of how many were by Vermeer himself, but such a stock must anyway have sat heavy on his accounts. We know he was invited to the Hague in 1672 to help authenticate some Italian paintings in the Uylenburg collection. He and a colleague from the guild refused authentication and Uylenburg bewailed that the value of rareties such as paintings had suffered a 'fall and decline in price in these calamitous times'. That Vermeer died poor and in debt in no way means that he was poor for most of this life. He could well have been a modestly prosperous dealer, as was his father, for whom painting may have been a passion but not an important source of income. When his fortunes collapsed in 1672 his response, according to Catharina, was not to paint more pictures but to stop painting altogether and concentrate on business. This is surely significant.

Vermeer's other income was from his wife's family. He moved some time after his marriage into the three-storey house owned and occupied by his mother-in-law, Maria Thins, in Delft's 'Papists' Corner'. He received money from Maria, and her family estate provided rental income for Catharina and their children. Maria may initially have opposed her daughter's marriage into a Protestant family but she appears to have warmed to Johannes in time. She cut her own son, Willem, out of most of the family estate in Catharina's favour and was devoted to the young man whom she called 'the sainted Vermeer' after his death. Vermeer named all his children after members of Maria Thins' family, never after his own. He called one of his sons Ignatius, which cannot have improved relations with the Calvinist Vermeers.

Montias's research shows a man strongly committed to his

adopted family circle. The imagination returns time and again to that crowded home on Oude Langendijck, to a young man who at 21 marries a Catholic girl of 22 against the wishes of both families, who changes his religion to make the marriage possible and moves out of his own secure family circle into the small Jesuit ghetto. His life must have been dominated by these two re-markable women, his mother-in-law Maria Thins, and his wife Catharina. The latter was almost always pregnant. She endured fifteen confinements in her twenty-two years of marriage to Johannes, eleven of which produced surviving children. These were not registered by the authorities and were probably baptized secretly.

Of all the facts known of Vermeer's life, the size of his family is the most extraordinary. Wealthy families in Holland at the time, Catholic as well as Protestant, were commonly limited to just two or three children. Simon Scharma has emphasized how developed was the literature of Dutch family planning and how important small families were to the character of Dutch society. Fewer chil-dren meant more money and less work for women. It also increased the attention paid to children. They were treasured and cossetted. Fathers played a public role in their upbringing that was quite new in Europe. Children featured prominently in paintings, not as appendages to posed portraits but as characters, actors in the restless game of Dutch genre.

Vermeer's unusually large family must have been intended. For Catharina to have been pregnant so persistently, right up to the year of Vermeer's death, suggests an intense marital bond, a father happy in his uxorious role and enjoying some financial security – a security that cannot have come from his output as a painter. The house must have had its tensions. Maria Thins was living in part of it and there is evidence of frequent trouble with Catharina's disturbed brother Willem, who threatened Catharina when she was pregnant. Yet this place became the principal source of inspi-ration for Vermeer's art: housework, letter-writing, entertaining, music-making. These may have been themes common to Dutch art at the time, but other artists varied their settings and subjects. They were not encompassed, as were all Vermeer's late works, within the walls of the home. Again I am forced back to my initial

149

supposition, that Vermeer's subjects and his treatment of them are most plausibly explained by his painting principally for himself, his family and close friends.

Are we any closer to *The Guitar Player*? That Vermeer liked portraying women is not in doubt. Apart from two landscapes and two, probably commissioned, male studies, every one of Vermeer's paintings features a woman. The identity of these subjects has passed relatively undiscussed by scholars more interested in speculating on Vermeer's technique and iconography. To them, if his art is essentially intellectual, of what relevance is the identity of his models? In addition, many of Vermeer's faces are of little significance to his composition. Some are almost sketches. Anybody could have modelled them.

We have no evidence that Vermeer did not use models. However, there is in my view a presumption that he did not, at least in his later work. His only two surviving male studies, *The Geographer* and *The Astronomer*, are generally accepted as portraits of the Delft scientist van Leeuwenhoek. Existing prints of him are strikingly similar to the Vermeer faces. The family maidservant, Tanneke Everpoel, is probably the model not just for the Amsterdam *Milkmaid* but also for the three other pictures in which a servant appears. The face, the physique and the clothes of this woman are identical in all four cases. For these paintings at least the artist appears to have used sitters from his immediate circle of family and friends.

So what of the remainder? The women portrayed in the remaining pictures, even the indistinct ones, all share a definite 'Vermeer' face. This face appears in at least twenty of his pictures, including the three apparently depicting a pregnant woman. These are not the idealized women of Italian art. They come across to us as real people, in keeping with the Dutch descriptive tradition. They have a strong family resemblance: high forehead, prominent jaw, straight nose, full cheeks, wide-set eyes and often a playful smile. This likeness applies both to the subjects that are clearly mature women and to those that look like young girls.

Once Vermeer had thrown off his first attempts at 'Italian' themes (possibly just four pictures), he turned to genre. In these new paintings there is a similarity not just in the faces of the ladies but also in their garments. I believe these garments offer clues – though not conclusive ones – in our investigation. From about 1659 to 1662, we see a young woman sometimes being entertained and even flirting with a succession of shadowy cavaliers. In the Dresden *Girl at a Window*, the Frick *Laughing Girl* and the Metropolitan's *Woman with a Water Jug*, she is wearing an identical blue and yellow bodice with striped sleeves. This distinctive outfit occurs again in the Buckingham Palace *Music Lesson* and the Boston *Concert*. It is not a thrown-on gown, as any model might be required to wear, but looks like the personal garment of a regular sitter. In the late 1660s, the subject changes into Vermeer's familiar yellow satin mantle with white fur trimmings listed in the inventory. This mantle would have been useful in concealing pregnancy and occurs in six pictures.

Catharina is often mentioned as the subject of the pregnancy pictures, if only for the improbability of a commercial model posing in such a condition. But if Catharina was sitting for the pregnancy studies, why not for the rest? Why go to the expense of hiring a model when an apparently willing wife is to hand, prepared to pose even when pregnant? Why go to the trouble of finding a model who looks so much like the Catharina of the pregnancy pictures and make her wear Catharina's garments? In the circumstances, I cannot see why we need to construct a 'commercial model' theory for Vermeer's studies of women. Nor is it surprising that we might be looking at Catharina in all Vermeer's pictures of mature women, given what we can reasonably conjecture of his family and of his love for his wife. But I do find such an identification offers an insight into his work. It suggests a deeper relationship with his subject matter than technical virtuosity or moral precept. It certainly makes more puzzling the enigma of Vermeer's genre: of Catharina entertaining or making music in the company of strangely anonymous men, or of her writing, sending and receiving letters. But the enigma is not resolved by retorting that no artist would portray his wife in such setting.

What of the daughters? The later pictures were allegedly painted round 1670, when Catharina was approaching the age of 40, though still bearing children. Swillens, one of the few scholars (with André Malraux) to discuss Vermeer's models, dismisses the thesis that those who are clearly young girls were his daughters on grounds of the girls' ages. He mistakenly believed the first-born to have been a son. We know from Montias that the Vermeers had four daughters before the arrival of a first son. The eldest was Maria, named after Vermeer's mother-in-law, probably born in 1554, within a year of the marriage. Elizabeth came next in 1657, then Cornelia and then Aleydis. Johannes did not appear before 1663. These girls were by no means too young to be models for Vermeer's later pictures. If Vermeer painted his wife so frequently, what could have been more natural than also to paint his daughters?

In only two pictures are we allowed to peer directly and at close hand into the eyes of a Vermeer model, the Hague *Girl with a Pearl Earring* and the Metropolitan *Head of a Girl* – to which I might add the generally attributed *Girl in a Red Hat* in Washington. I believe all these could be portraits of Vermeer's daughters. In each case the portrayal is startling. The Metropolitan portrait is direct, almost mesmerizing. The Hague one, probably five years earlier, is among one of the most moving evocations of the human face in Dutch art. Vermeer emerges from these pictures not as the cold practitioner of Dutch genre but as an intensely intimate portraitist. These faces do not have the sexual content or emotional engagement that Proust so missed in Vermeer's work. This is hardly surprising if they are a father's study of his teenage daughters.

The faces are distinct yet similar enough to be members of the same family. Their dark, wide-set eyes are even reminiscent of those of the man on the left of Vermeer's early *Procuress*, long regarded as a self-portrait. Their open faces and even features also have much in common with those of their mother, Catharina. We can surmise that they would be the two eldest girls, Maria and Elizabeth. But can conjecture be taken any further than this? If we accept the dating of the Hague girl at roughly 1665–6, Maria would then have been 11 or 12 and Elizabeth 9 or 10. Either age could apply to this enchanting young face but Maria must be the more likely. A remarkably similar face appears as the demure young girl sitting for her father in Vermeer's masterpiece in Vienna, *The Art of Painting*. Here an artist dressed in medieval costume, assumed to be Vermeer himself, is shown painting a portrait of a girl with garlands in her hair. Like almost all Vermeer's works, the picture is an imitation of (or was inspired by) pictures of similar themes by his contemporaries. Here he has adapted an anonymous genre scene to show a Renaissance artist portraying a child. The other portrait, in the Metropolitan, has been dated to eight years later than the Hague one. Since the two portraits do not appear to be of the same girl, if Maria is in the Hague then Elizabeth must be in the Metropolitan. At this point, caution suggests we leave these pictures in peace.

Let us move to the face that stares out at us from the two virginals players in London's National Gallery and from the religious *Allegory of Faith* in New York's Metropolitan. These faces, though mature, are manifestly not Catharina. The face and figure of the model shows a stout woman, in the *Allegory* positively fat, with strong Vermeer eyes and swept-back hair. In all three pictures she is identically clad, in a rich blue dress, with white sleeves and pearls round a plump neck. Like Catharina's early bodice, this costume does not look like the drapes an artist would put on a model, more items of personal clothing. In each case, the hair is drawn back and given a fringe of wispy curls. The iconography suggests that the pictures were executed as a pair and at much the same time.

Let us assume this to be Maria again, Vermeer's eldest daughter now grown from the Hague portrait of a decade earlier and approaching the date of her marriage in 1674. Once again I find the garment significant. The blue dress with white sleeves does not appear in Catharina's inventory of Vermeer's posthumous belongings. These dresses would have been possessions of great value. The famous yellow fur-trimmed jacket and also the blue pregnancy jacket are both in the inventory. We know that Maria married a year before Vermeer's death, and would naturally have taken the blue dress with her to her new house. Since almost everything Vermeer painted – chairs, pictures, jugs, carpets, personal garments – occurs in the inventory, the absence of the blue dress offers strong circumstantial evidence for the blue-dressed model being Maria. In addition, the virginals would have been the most important instrument of family music-making, the continuo, and would most naturally have been played by the eldest daughter.

So what of the guitarist, among Vermeer's last pictures? She is surely too young to be Catharina. She does not look like the girl in blue standing or seated at the family virginals. She is wearing her mother's old yellow jacket, strumming chords on the guitar. The most likely candidate must be the next daughter, Elizabeth. But are there other clues? The distinctive look, those strong dark eyes and high brow are certainly similar to those of the Metropolitan portrait, which I have tentatively identified as Elizabeth and which experts believe was painted at roughly the same time. The hairstyle (with plait and faintly Rastafarian ringlets) is identical to that of the girl in the same yellow jacket in the Louvre *Lacemaker*. *The Lacemaker* shares with *The Guitar Player* the distinction of being the only authenticated Vermeers lit from the right rather than the left. At the probable time of painting, Elizabeth could have been anywhere between 15 and 17. She is portrayed here as fresher, certainly less plump, than her elder sister. She is not the poised, responsible eldest child just two years from matrimony, but still a tender teenager, dreaming of courtship.

We know at least something of this picture. After Vermeer's death, Catharina strove even amid bankruptcy to keep hold of three of his works. One was the *Art of Painting* mentioned above and probably painted a decade before *The Guitar Player*. To this picture Catharina was especially attached. When she went bankrupt she ceded it to her mother-in-law in payment of a family debt as a way of keeping it from other creditors. The other two favoured pictures were the Beit *Woman with her Maid* and *The Guitar Player*. Soon after Vermeer's death, Catharina was forced to give these two pictures to the local baker, van Buyten, in payment of a large debt. But the agreement said that he should not dispose of either work. If Catharina was later able to pay the original debt in cash, he would return them. He agreed this 'after being seriously beseeched' by Catharina, indeed upon her 'urgent persistence'.

These pictures must have had a particular significance for Catharina. I find it hard to believe that the reason for her attachment to them lay in some ideological or moral message. Rather it must have lain in what they portrayed: the first, her husband painting their eldest child; the second, herself and her maid Tanneke; and the third, Elizabeth at the guitar. Is it any wonder that she sought to keep hold of these three works in her darkest period? As Swillens says, 'Her efforts bear witness to a great love and sacrifice.'

The Guitar Player is an uncharacteristically joyful work. Most of Vermeer's women seem locked in time and place, permitted escape only through the medium of his brush. Some are writing or reading letters, coyly looking at the viewer or communing some secret to a maid. Round them are the objects of the household, balancing scales, water jugs, maps and globes. Vermeer's iconography has yielded a vast corpus of investigation, but the icons in *The Guitar Player* are few. There is a bare room, a table with a shawl and some books, a richly framed landscape, possibly a van der Velde from Vermeer's stock. And there is the instrument, sometimes called a cittern or long-stemmed guitar.

We have seen that music-making was an important part of Vermeer family life. In the alleged self-portrait of Vermeer in *The Procuress*, he is shown holding a similar instrument. In the *Art of Painting* Maria holds a trombone. A musical instrument appears in ten Vermeers, a third of his known output. In most cases they are playing little by way of music. The instrument is a silent witness, a mere prop, part of the furniture of middle-class life. The musicians, whether Catharina or Maria, have stopped playing. They appear to have been interrupted by the artist, asked to pose and keep still. No tunes rise from the keyboard or hover in the air. All is silence. The only playing is that of light and shade, of sun and shadow.

Not so *The Guitar Player*. Proust cannot have seen this picture. Here for once there is a song on the lips of a Vermeer woman. A tune is dancing from the girl's fingers. Her eyes are certainly distracted but she continues to sing. There is animation in the face and body. Nor is this the only unusual feature of the work. Vermeer remains the experimenter, perhaps even discarding his camera obscura. Whereas previously he was prepared to move his model deep into his perspective, here he does something quite different, he moves her to one side. The focus is thrown off centre. The artist both alerts and distracts our attention. Like a painter of the baroque, he seizes the viewer's gaze and turns it to the left of the canvas. The eye passes first to the hand on the guitar, then along the arm to the shoulder and forehead, then into the eyes. These eyes are in shadow, yet they are vital, the spark of the canvas. These are true Vermeer eyes. They are alert to the world around them, asking us to guess what they see and for what they are hoping. They do not rest, but lead us out of the frame, off into the distance towards some unseen individual or object. Every time I look at this remarkable face I wonder, At what was she looking?

The restlessness does not stop there. The model's right arm is cut off uncomfortably, almost as if the canvas had later been chopped. (It has not: this is a rare Vermeer still on its original stretcher.) The model's right knee beneath her dress is raised towards us and foreshortened. This lends a sudden movement, almost a rhythm, to the composition. Vermeer repeated this feature identically in the *Allegory of Faith* – unless the imitation was the other way round. This is Vermeer at his most untypical. The paint is laid on not in the subtle gradations of his early work, but in patches. The boundaries between yellows and whites and greys are sharply defined across the folds in the dress and the curls of the hair. The play of light, coming unusually from the right of the room, is dappled across the subject. The light source itself is uncertain. The window is curtained and the glimpse of day showing through it cannot yield the vivid shadows given to the girl's head and the frame behind her. Some critics have found this crude, indicating a degeneration in Vermeer's craft. I see it as the artist still the technical experimenter. Either way, I cannot believe it was intended for a patron or the Delft art market.

Writers on Vermeer seldom avoid some expression of bafflement. Why, asks Swillens, 'if he wished to indulge his passion for colour, did he paint no flowers? Why if he wished to reveal the wonderful play of light, no landscape bathed in sunlight? Why no children when he saw them round him daily?' Lawrence Gowing wonders at the aura of 'activity interrupted' in Vermeer's pictures. He sees him detached from his subjects, hidden behind a thick curtain in the camera obscura box: 'a world of ideal, undemanding relationships. There he could spend hours watching the silent women move to and fro . . . He could record them and from the uncertainty he could distil something miraculously definite, pure and absolute.' Even the admirable Montias writes of Vermeer's 'intimate urgings that prompted him to paint . . . pensive women pent up in shallow spaces'. There is no shortage of conjecture, but all directed at seeing Vermeer as the lone genius of Delft art.

I have come to see a different Vermeer. I see a contented family man, certainly committed to his calling as painter but primarily a dealer, *rentier* and Catholic paterfamilias, his work inspired by his love for his wife and ever growing family, mostly of girls. He was respected by fellow artists, but did not paint much and what he painted might have seemed at the time derivative in subject matter and concerned chiefly with the optical innovations of his friend, the scientist van Leeuwenhoek. His paintings, if they circulated at all, went to connoisseurs such as van Ruijven.

Thus far I agree with Gowing: Vermeer is not an enigma but the victim of one. He is eternally at the mercy of those who seek to probe his mind. But if conjecture there is to be, let us join Swillens in taking him down from his pedestal and placing him in his domestic context, conversing with his wife and daughters in his studio while he plays his variations on a theme of light and shadow. Catharina bustles back and forth, beautiful and entrancing. She is everywhere, writing, playing, entertaining, mothering, giving birth. She gazes out at us from the portrait in the Frick with a warmth and realism that suggests no commercial model. How crucial was she to his genius? Is she not entitled to recognition, to a sort of immortality?

Her daughter Maria was granted her own memorial, serene but severe, standing at the virginals every inch the eldest child. But Elizabeth? Let her be the singer, perhaps her father's favourite, strumming her guitar while he painted. She consoled Vermeer after Maria had married and left and was as distraught as her mother when he suddenly died. She too has her immortality. She is singing still, up there on the heights of Hampstead. I sometimes feel on a cold afternoon that I could take her by the hand and walk her out across the Heath, trying not to ask her all those myriad Vermeer questions, asking her only to keep singing. If I ever do, I promise her a better resting place than that dank Smithfield graveyard.

19

LEONARDO ON HIGH

To Oxford to see a picture being hung. Not any picture, but the unveiling of a long-lost treasure, the Royal Academy copy of Leonardo's *Last Supper*. The copy was made, possibly by Leonardo's follower Gianpietrino, at the same time as the original fresco in the church of Santa Maria delle Grazie in Milan. The Academy acquired it in 1821 for students to use as a model but had long left it in store for want of a suitable wall on which to hang it. In 1992 the canvas work was rolled round a huge drum and gingerly moved from the Academy by truck up the M40 to Magdalen College chapel. The result was a brilliant alliance of art and architecture and one that merited celebration. Celebration it duly received, from the assembled Fellows of Magdalen in March 1993. All the arts were mustered to the glory of this painting. Never again will I hang a picture by merely banging a nail into a wall.

Great architecture imposes its own character on an occasion. The stones of Magdalen, grey or honey-coloured, Gothic or Classical, were the backdrop to our ceremony. The evening began at 4.30 with the painting lit high on the wall of the antechapel, positioned so as to emphasize the perspective and foreshortening of Leonardo's composition. Some 400 visitors gazed up in awe. Then the art historian Sir Ernst Gombrich delivered a magisterial lecture on Leonardo and on the Milan fresco. Sadly, his thick Viennese phrases were lost to most listeners amid the Gothic vaults of the chapel, yet they infused the occasion with an intellectual beatitude.

There followed tea in the Hall and a candlelit evensong back in the chapel, a service rich in copes, bishops and incense. Twenty-eight choristers sung an anthem composed by Magdalen's choir-master, Grayston Ives, in honour of the painting. The Bishop of Winchester, Visitor of the college, blessed the new acquisition and bade us see it as 'a place of rest and peace on our earthly pilgrimage'. We then processed to dinner in Hall by the traditional Fellows' route over the roofs of the Cloisters, steeped in dark Gothic shadows. We heard the Secretary of the Royal Academy, Piers Rodgers, tell of the picture's life since it left Leonardo's workshop, of its passage to the Charterhouse of Pavia and then via the Continental art market into the hands of the Academy. We drank its health in Sauterne and college port. The evening ended with a last glimpse of the masterpiece, unsleeping, radiant on its chapel wall.

The marriage of Leonardo and Magdalen was the result of a delightful serendipity. A college Fellow, Professor Colin Blakemore, overheard Rodgers bewailing the lack of a 'good wall' on which to hang his picture. Blakemore and the college President, Anthony Smith, knew that they had just such an empty wall, high in their antechapel. Indeed they had been pondering asking the Academy for a different copy, of a Raphael, to put there. Delicate negotiations ensued and the picture was eventually secured on long-term loan. Olivetti paid for its restoration in Milan, by the same team as had restored the original fresco. American friends of the college paid for the removal and rehanging.

Anthony Smith was rightly proud of his acquisition. He wished to pay it respect in a manner that appealed to his own sense of ceremony. Gombrich's discourse was beguiling even where inaudible. Lasting almost an hour, it was itself a damaged fresco, its fragments emerging intermittently from the gloom to reveal the master's genius. Admirers of Gombrich's *Story of Art* will know that he regards *The Last Supper* as simply 'one of the great miracles wrought by human genius'. Here, he said, was Leonardo 'in contest with Giotto'. Here was Leonardo straining to represent 'both man and the intentions of man'. Here was Leonardo portraying bodily movement round the formal setting of a Renaissance dining-room. The impetuous artist even departed from strict fresco technique and applied oil-based pigment to the wall surface – tragically condemning his masterpiece to early deterioration.

Gombrich quoted Goethe, to whom *The Last Supper* was the 'coping stone of Western art'. He quoted Lord Clark who, on first confronting it, was 'appalled at the quantity of writing which this masterpiece has evoked'. Clark added, 'Almost more numbing than this authority is its familiarity. How can we criticise a work which we have all known from childhood? We have come to regard Leonardo's *Last Supper* more as a work of nature than a work of man, and we no more think of questioning its shape than we should question the shape of the British Isles on the map.' In the popular imagination, the picture has been seen as the authentic portrayal of a biblical incident. Here is the moment when, according to the Bible, Christ told the shocked disciples that one of them would betray him. They reply as one, 'Lord, is it I?'

I have not seen the damaged Milan fresco, which has recently been restored to remove overpainting that had all but ruined its appearance. But reproductions suggest that this copy displays a detail and a vitality lost from the original. It is especially precious. Whatever the critics of art reproduction may say, this is a splendid vindication of the copyist's craft, a message across time of the master's intention and inspiration. Scientific tests have proved it to be contemporary with the original fresco. Whether Leonardo himself supervised the work, whether he may even have executed some of it himself, is not known. We can only see the evidence before us, and imagine his assistants inspired and galvanized into producing a true 'Leonardo'. There is about the work none of the 'glib prettiness' that Berenson decried in the work of Leonardo's Milan followers.

Above all the work demonstrates Gombrich's reiterated emphasis on Leonardo's realism. It shows his fascination with optics, dynamics, anatomy, the motion of the body, the expression of the face. The foreshortening of the figures of the disciples, when lit from above, makes them seem to move about the canvas, as if about to kick over the table in their anguish. Gombrich found them so lifelike as to permit himself one modest joke, that today they would be called an exercise in 'virtual reality'. As for their exaggerated hand gestures, he pointed out that this was 'plainly an Italian supper'. The picture is unframed and might almost be a *trompe-l'œil*: an opening in the chapel wall giving us a glimpse of a college feast, with the gardens of North Oxford transformed into an exotic landscape through windows in the distance.

Music's contribution to the occasion, in the form of Ives's anthem, was wholly appropriate. Enhanced by a hundred flickering candles, the singing echoed the picture's drama and accessibility. The trebles uttered Christ's accusation of betrayal. The tenors and basses returned the terrified response: 'Lord, is it I?' Their voices rose into the vaults of the antechapel and hovered round the heads of the disciples. Beneath was an audience of candlelit faces, clerics, scholars, students, passers-by from the street outside. The architecture, the lighting, the costumes of the choristers, even the cadences of the music, were in harmony with the picture. Our twentieth-century clothes seemed incongruous.

This was indeed a celebration of incongruities: a Renaissance painting hung in a Gothic chapel, blessed by a Teutonic lecturer amid a High Anglican ritual. But the contrasts were more apparent than real. This was a Renaissance anniversary. It is exactly half a millennium since Leonardo conceived *The Last Supper*. He first climbed the scaffolding in Santa Maria delle Grazie in 1494 and completed the work four years later, shortly before he resumed roaming the courts of Europe. Also in 1494 William Orchard, master mason of English late Gothic, would have been climbing the scaffolding round Magdalen Tower, then rising over the roof of his great cloister. Orchard had completed the chapel itself in 1480 (its interior was rebuilt in 1828). Was this cultural coincidence without significance? Can we not see Gothic and Renaissance here fused in a vivid work of humanism?

The buildings of English late Perpendicular were rich and inventive manifestations of an art that was far from grim or medieval. Leonardo's heads of St Peter and Judas, copied in this picture, might have been borrowed from one of Orchard's Magdalen gargoyles. The Oxford of this period was as splendid as the court of any Italian prince. It found its apotheosis in Orchard's ceiling of the Divinity Schools next to the Bodleian Library, and in his cloister and tower at Magdalen. He himself was commissioned to design the chapel's west window and the cloister windows, 'as good as or better than those of All Souls College'. He was no mere technician. He was rewarded for his artistry with college rents and land in Headington, for which he paid with a red rose once a year. Nor was Orchard the only Renaissance man to frequent Magdalen at this time. In the same year that Leonardo finally completed his fresco, 1498, Magdalen acted as host to Erasmus. The future Cardinal Wolsey was then the college bursar. The President of the college at the time of Orchard's building, Richard Mayew, was a senior figure of state and confidant of Henry VII, from whom the college received its statutes and much of its land and future wealth.

Tudor Magdalen was no academic *ultima Thule*, cut off from the smile of reason beaming down on Rome and Florence. It was, albeit briefly, a centre of Europe's artistic and intellectual rebirth. Here in Oxford, now as then, was a harmony of art and architecture, of Gothic and Renaissance, of learning and music. That March evening I fell to wondering how many other such suitors were waiting in galleries, vaults and historic houses across Britain, needing only someone of imagination and enterprise to bring them together. Paintings are not meant to be herded into galleries. They are best seen, like beautiful buildings or music, in a setting that befits their original inspiration. It is only the grandiosity of donors and the acquisitiveness of curators that condemns them to life in a museum. There should be a cultural Royal Exchange to bring pictures and buildings into fruitful union. Magdalen and the Royal Academy have shown the way.

20

CINDERELLA GEOGRAPHY

I NEVER studied proper geography. The last lesson in the subject that I recall was at the age of 12 and concerned the production of soap in Peru. I went to an academic secondary school. I did the required number of O-levels, none of which was geography. For me the curricular Earth was still flat. At its centre stood the Classics, maths and English. History was at the outer edge. Geography had vanished completely.

My acquaintance with the subject was renewed during the debate that took place – or was supposed to take place – in the late 1980s over curriculum reform. The New Geography as it was called was a revelation. The subject had emerged from the obscurity of its atlases and lists of rivers into the light of day and into contemporary relevance. My son found it constantly topical, filling out the images that he caught fragmentarily on television or in newspapers: famine, environmental damage, the redrawing of national boundaries, arguments over motorways. Geography challenged him, made him question his surroundings. His topic work included conservation, food supply, space travel, energy sources, town planning, the development of home, school and workplace. Here was a discipline that took him out of the classroom into the world and said, 'Look what's here! How did it come to be? What is it made of and who did it?'

Perhaps I am drawn to underdogs. It shocked me that geography was not a compulsory foundation subject for GCSE in the government's new curriculum but was regarded as interchangeable with history. What could it mean, interchangeable with history, when the two were part of the same intellectual framework? Geography was forced to lurk in the shadows not just of maths, English and science but even of such newly fashionable subjects as technology. Nothing is by its nature more conservative than education. Nothing in education is more conservative than curriculum. And nothing in curriculum is more conservative than the fixation with Great Subjects. But if great subjects there must be, surely one of them should be the study of the planet?

Like all searches in education this one leads to the ivy-clad walls of the old universities, institutions that embody scholastic conservatism. There the Big Three have deep roots. The emphasis on English, maths and science reflects not some argued educational theory but simply an updating of medieval pursuits. It lies in a belief, prevalent in much professional training, that the more abstruse the learning, the better the mental discipline. I recall a scholar once claiming that the world's greatest minds had been honed on the exclusive study of a single text: the Bible, Cicero, the Talmud, the Koran. 'Liberal studies' were the death of genius. The mental lyre can never be strung too tight. I have yet to find a shred of evidence for this theory. Yet it is repeated by otherwise sensible people and underpins debate on the curriculum across much of Europe.

As recently as the 1960s I was taught nothing from the age of 15 to 17 but Latin, Greek and Classical history. My school considered these the most prestigious subjects for its sixth form and directed its brightest pupils (so I was told) in their direction. The Classics were the sure basis on which to gain entry to the best universities. At Oxford they were honoured with the title of Greats. This status was in line of descent from the monastic education of the Middle Ages. Even Arnold of Rugby, regarded as a leading reformer, dared not infringe it. Arnold transformed the moral standing of the English public school, but not its curriculum. Lytton Strachey wrote, 'He deliberately adhered to the old system. The monastic and literary conceptions of education, which had their roots in the Middle Ages, . . . he adopted almost without hesitation. Under him the public school remained in essentials a conventional establishment devoted to the teaching of Greek and Latin grammar.' In retrospect this was a devastating opportunity lost, from which some might say British education and training never recovered. At the time, German technical education was surging ahead. Such was Arnold's ascendancy, said Strachey, that he could have recast the school curriculum along modern lines. 'As it was, he threw the whole weight of his influence into the opposite scale, and the ancient system became more firmly established than ever.'

That system survived to my own day. From the age of 15, I studied no history or geography, no politics or economics, no art and no science, nothing to guide my uncertain steps in an uncertain world. This was possibly a source of pride to my teachers. It was as if the impracticality and purity of the Classics were a measure of their value. They did not challenge the intellectual fortress of the staffroom with direct contact with the world outside. Let that world enter a classroom and in might rush controversy, subjectivity and argument. This aversion was rooted in fear. Children should be taught 'what we know'; it is easier for teachers and comforting for parents. I believe many teachers, weak ones, have always sought the pedagogical equivalent of a doctor's Greek prescriptions or a lawyer's Latin aphorisms. The educated need a distance from the uneducated, the professional from the lay, the insider from the mass. A hundred years after Arnold, the bias towards Classics has ended in British secondary schools. My subjects of Latin and Greek have sunk down the national curriculum. (I wonder what Promethean battle of the deities led to this fall from grace.) They had survived an astonishing half millennium since the Renaissance. But their precursor in the pantheon of ancient learning, geography, has not been the beneficiary. I wonder why.

A recent bestseller, *The Discoverers*, by the Librarian of Congress, Daniel Boorstin, opens with a eulogy to the early Greek geographers. Theirs was the true science, the highest achievement of the intellect. They were the first to challenge the mythologists and storytellers by pointing to the world about them, the first to use fact to challenge legend. Men such as Eratosthenes, Strabo and Ptolemy observed, enquired, recorded. They discovered, or at least deduced, the central fact of science, that the world was round. In the third century BC, Eratosthenes went farther. He compared the shadows of the sun at different times of day and year in upper and lower Egypt and calculated the circumference of the globe. He was only 15 per cent out. One of learning's great mistakes was Ptolemy's recalculation of Eratosthenes' work in the second century AD, reducing the Earth's circumference by half. Thirteen centuries later, Columbus relied on Ptolemy and went searching for Genghis Khan in the highlands of central Cuba; Boorstin points out that, had he relied on Eratosthenes, he would never have set sail. If the fifteenth century had known that China was three times farther west than it thought, the European settlement of America would probably have awaited the age of steam.

What concerned Boorstin, and should concern us, is what happened to geography after Ptolemy. The answer was the Roman Church. Between the second and fifteenth centuries AD, Ptolemy's geography and his zest for discovery were driven underground. For over a thousand years the search for knowledge about the world ceased and discovery was forced into retreat. This was the Great Interruption. A blanket of dogma descended on the empirical tradition that had flourished round the Mediterranean under the Roman empire. No other civilization took up the torch of knowledge, not Arabia nor China. For all of Christendom, Jerusalem had to be the centre of the earth because Ezekiel said so. The wisdom of the elders was to be received and not challenged.

Boorstin concludes:

Geography had no place in the medieval catalogue of seven arts: the quadrivium of mathematical disciplines, arithmetic, music, geometry and astronomy, and the trivium of liberal disciplines, grammar, dialectic and rhetoric. For a thousand years no synonym for geography was in ordinary usage. The word did not enter the English language until the mid-sixteenth century. Lacking the dignity of a proper discipline, geography was an orphan in the world of learning. The subject became a ragbag filled with odds and ends of knowledge and pseudo-knowledge, of biblical dogmas, travellers' tales, philosophers' speculations and mythical imaginings.

Even the cartographers, those master mariners of early discovery, were whipped into line. We find it near incredible that Ptolemy's maps, with coasts and rivers overlaid by the lines of early longitude and latitude, were a millennium before not after the Hereford *mappa mundi*. The latter was a crude attempt to equate the world reported by travellers to a world ordained by biblical scholars. The biblical world was divided between the sons of Noah and surrounded by Heaven and Hell. The empiricism of Ptolemy had been put to flight by the images of Hieronymous Bosch.

Not until the fifteenth century did mariners dare to record their discoveries of new seas and new shorelines in map form. They did so primarily for the help and safety of their fellow sailors. If what they saw with their own eyes conflicted with what religion taught them, experience told them to trust their eyes. Copernicus, Galileo and Erasmus might be questioning other tenets of theology, but simple sailors led the revival of Ptolemaic geography. In the mid-fifteenth century, Henry the Navigator reviewed the ancient maps and set about improving them. The seas, winds and currents were facts free of dogma, free for thought and questioning, free for adventure. The renaissance of geography and cartography thus lay in the needs of ordinary men. It was a practical not an intellectual imperative.

The schoolmen fought back. At first the Inquisition persecuted map-makers. No charts of Columbus's discoveries were produced for more than a decade after his first voyage. Not until 1507 did Waldseemuller print his first map of America. The great Mercator was regarded as a dangerous fanatic. Rounded up with forty-two Flanders heretics, he watched as two were burned alive, two buried alive and one beheaded. Mercator escaped but did not dare publish his famous projection until 1569. The Inquisition was supported by monarchs jealous of the commercially useful intelligence brought back by mariners. Maps were state secrets which rulers kept in their private closets. To know the outline of a new continent was to hold the keys to great wealth. In Spain and Portugal geography was equated with espionage. Map-makers and their documents were guarded and poached, like nuclear scientists in the Cold War. Even today historians are not sure whether the Portuguese reached America before Columbus, as they know the Vikings did. A secret is only safe if the fact of its existence is also a secret. Not until the publication of Ortelius's atlas in 1570 was a gentleman able to put the world in his pocket and discuss it with his friends.

The universities, still under the influence of the Church, never relented. Geography may have won its revival in the admiralties, trading companies and publishing houses of Europe, but not in the universities. Religion and its dogmas still dominated most academic thought, whether that of the Reformation or the Counter-Reformation. While the Roman Catholic Church was condemning Galileo, Luther was dismissing Copernicus: 'This fool', he said, 'wishes to reverse the entire science of astronomy. Scripture tells us that Joshua commanded the sun to stand still, not the Earth.' University scholars were guardians of an intellectual closed shop, not innovators, explorers or discoverers. Through their training of teachers, universities also determined what was taught in schools. They were education's oligarchs. Thus the national curriculum began its march down the ages and into the subconscious of Britain's Department of Education.

Let me not exaggerate. Not all the disciplines of the medieval university have retained their primacy, nor was geography totally ignored. Greek, Latin and divinity have suffered near total eclipse. Among the former liberal arts, logic, dialectic and rhetoric have been neglected – as any student of politics is aware. Grammar has fared better, living on in the dominance of English language studies. Arithmetic, geometry and astronomy have retained their eminence, reflected in the foundation status of mathematics and science. But the subject that was pre-eminent before the Great Interruption never recovered its former glory. Geography still shivers in the shadow of the Inquisition.

When some years ago I wrote an article deploring geography's low university ranking I was surprised at the response. Senior academics were patronizing. Yes indeed, geography needed a pat on the head, but not at the expense of 'proper subjects'. At the same time, distinguished citizens took me aside to confide that they had themselves studied the subject but were usually embarrassed to admit it. I had chanced upon an oppressed fraternity. Geography was a secret stigma. This lack of self-confidence was reflected in the attitudes of teachers, in the standing of geography departments in schools, in the academic career advice given by teachers to pupils. Once trapped in an academic vicious circle, a subject finds it hard to escape, especially after two thousand years of neglect.

The clue to a subject's status is how it fares in the timetable against its rivals. Only history is as poorly treated as geography, though its university status is higher. The education secretary in 1991, Kenneth Clarke, said portentously that 'a firm foundation in physical geography is essential if young people are to understand the physical nature of the world in which they live and the consequences of the interactions between people and the physical environment. Good geography should act as a counter against superficial and semi-formed opinions.' The reiteration of the word 'physical' was, of course, code. To an education politician, physical means objective, by way of contrast with social or subjective. Mr Clarke was against such dangerous mutants as social geography. These sentiments did not lead him to give geography a higher ranking in the curriculum. To me the test was whether geography should stand alongside, and perhaps even supplant, mathematics, science or English in the core. Should it at least rank with technology as a foundation subject? The answer was no.

I can see that children should be taught grammar, to read and write, to count and assess proportion. But why should they learn these things through the medium of English, maths and science rather than, say, as tools to the understanding of history, economics or geography? Beyond the most basic literacy and numeracy skills, these subjects have come to be treated as 'cores' largely because the teaching profession has so determined, not from any intrinsic value in the subjects themselves. Their very impracticality seems to lend them academic status. Yet a school can surely give a child no greater gift than to understand the story of its surroundings, from the neighbourhood of home, to the town, the nation, the planet and the universe. Such teaching must be closer to true education, the 'leading out' of a mind, than differential equations, the composition of the atom or the reproduction of an amoeba.

English, maths and science are seen by teachers as holding the keys to some notional door of the intellect – as were the Bible and Latin to Arnold. In the case of maths and science, this door (when pushed open) reveals nothing to do with the intellectual health of the individual. It derives from a concern for the nation's prosperity: 'The country needs more scientists and mathematicians.' This is a normative assumption, that science-based industry must lie at the heart of Britain's future wealth. What about languages, or accountancy, or law, or economics? How do such assumptions come to dominate the curriculum? Or is the truth of the matter that academic scientists and mathematicians wish for a constant supply of new recruits to their departments, to keep them in graduate students and research scholars? This was how the Classics dominated education from the sixteenth century far into the twentieth. Science and mathematics have picked up the same torch. Nobody thinks what best to teach those not destined for an academic career.

To argue publicly for the study of the nature of the Earth before that of maths or science is to experience Galileo's fate before the Inquisition. Maths is holy writ. Curriculum planners have ignored the coming of the pocket calculator and the irrelevance of maths to most pupils in later life. (Beyond elementary arithmetic, economics would be a far more sensible 'numerate' core subject.) I believe part of its appeal to teachers and parents is its apparent objectivity. In maths, the teacher need brook no argument. Geography is an invitation to argue. Like equally suspect history, it is licensed subjectivity. The new geography has expanded from maps and climate to embrace many of the social and environmental sciences, as well as economic history. It has become relevant to current affairs, to political debate. It encourages young people to question the world about them, and question what their teachers are telling them. It is Socratic: 'The unquestioned life is not worth living.' That is why politicians appeal to those most conservative educationists, parents, for support against geographical innovation. 'Stick to mountains and rivers!' they cry. Stick to sums and algebra.

A recent book, *The End of Geography* by R. O'Brien, pointed out that information technology had broken down all geographical barriers. Computers had brought Brussels close to Manhattan and Tokyo to London. Jets had done the same for tourism, container ships for trade. The fax and the mobile phone had torn up time-tables and shrunk distances to nothing. The globe was a village. We had no need of geography. I cannot imagine a sillier prediction. The modern world is too fast for such futurology. What I know is that the atlas on my desk is rarely closed. Where are the boundaries of Serbia? Are the Armenians Europeans? How far is Hong Kong from Guangzhou? What are the 'water wars' of the Middle East? Need the Sahel starve? Where is the ozone layer? These are questions which today's master mariners must be equipped to answer. They embrace discoveries awaiting every young person. Many are political and controversial, many are not susceptible to factual answer. They demand enquiry, argument and debate. That is their value to education. Geography is alive and well. Rarely, it seems, does it go to school.

21

DR SYNTAX AND
MRS GRUNDY

WINSTON CHURCHILL did not doubt the key to his success. When at Harrow, he said, he was regarded as stupid and was therefore demoted to a class that studied no Latin or Greek. He studied only grammar. As a result, he said, 'I got into my bones the essential structure of the normal British sentence – which is a noble thing.' He exploited it to the full. He became master of its metaphor, its cadence and its rhythm. He put sentences to the purpose of politics. They never failed him. If words could win a war, his did. I have always been intrigued by Churchill's command of language, as it seemed instinctive rather than learnt. I now know better. He was taught to write and speak English and taught well.

For a brief period in the 1980s, Her Majesty's Secretary of State for Education was Kenneth Baker. He was what might in Churchill's day have been called a 'card'. His career appeared to be a series of débâcles, yet he would emerge from each one sleek-groomed and smiling, as if eager for the next. He became court jester to Margaret Thatcher in some of her blacker moments. She would tease him and make him the butt of her private ridicule. Perhaps for this reason, she regarded him as an indispensable ingredient in her grey cabinet gruel.

Mr Baker was as keen on grammar as was Churchill. Grammar was to him an 'issue', a base metal out of which political gold might be created. He and Mrs Thatcher treated grammar as a potent electoral topic, like crime or dole fraud. English literature was, in comparison, effete and dangerous. No matter that most Tory workers loathed the subject, nor that most ministers had little obvious command of it. Grammar stirred the political juices. Grammar was the intellectual equivalent of the cane and the birch. With this in mind Mr Baker commissioned a report on the teaching of grammar from a professor, Brian Cox, considered sound as co-author of a 'Black Paper' on education. Professor Cox submitted a sensible, indeed unexceptionable, report. But he included in it a passage suggesting that greater emphasis be placed on reading and oral expression – called 'oracy' – than on written work. He also made a slighting reference to formal grammar teaching and to those who regarded Standard English as a 'prestige dialect'. Professor Cox hails from Lancashire.

No sooner had the Cox report broken cover than Mr Baker disowned it. He seized his twelve-bore from the gun-room, raised it to his shoulder and blasted away in full hearing of the press. 'I believe you can't actually communicate well as a young person unless you understand the structure of the language,' he thundered (with a redundant 'actually'). Far from accepting the Professor's suggestion, Mr Baker said he was ordering his officials 'to give greater emphasis to the pupils' mastery of the grammatical structure of the English language'. The Conservative party and press roared their approval. Worried teachers wondered what it all meant. The only reassurance the education department could give was that, despite Mr Baker's remarks, 'there would be no immediate return to parsing or clause analysis'.

Why not? I wondered. Those for whom words are the raw material of daily life, which means every non-manual worker, ought to have given Mr Baker a cheer. The writing produced by most modern schools and universities is dreadful. Application letters for jobs, a litmus test of educational standards, are often illiterate. At *The Times* we used to struggle to ensure the editorial pages were spelled correctly, but the advertisements were beyond our control and in chaos. We expect an engineering student to know some maths and a music student to know scales. We cannot expect young people who will spend their lives composing sentences, spoken and written, to go into the world not knowing how to do it. They are expected to handle letters and memorandums, public-speaking, word processing, computer programming. How can they do this without knowing the basics of English grammar? Grammar is not a ritual, a code drawn up simply to help bright pupils get places at good universities. It holds the key to clear communication and gainful employment.

I do not think that British literacy is in irreversible decline. More people read books, take serious newspapers, write prose and poetry than ever before. Only letter-writing is in decline, and that was inevitable with the advent of the telephone (though I understand that the fax has given letters a new lease of life). Many of these 'new literates' were taught English in the 1960s and '70s, derided by the New Right as education's dark ages. Some teachers regarded grammar as a bourgeois shackle on a child's cultural identity. To them, grammar was for a mandarin élite. Ordinary people said what they meant and said it straight.

Jared Diamond's *Rise and Fall of the First Chimpanzee* gives the lie to this approach. He discusses early grammars and compares them with the noises, bordering on words, that can be taught to monkeys. Scholars now believe that human babies, unlike those of monkeys, are genetically programmed to use grammar, to order words into sentences. But the sentences they form are simplified 'creole' ones, in effect baby talk. Such primitive grammars must be overridden by the more complicated ones that have arisen where a number of root languages have combined, as is the case with English. This may explain the difficulty that many foreigners, and many children, have with the word order of English negative and interrogative sentences. Such grammar has to be learnt. To deny pupils instruction in it is to deny them a vital life skill.

The *Oxford English Dictionary* defines a sentence as 'a series of words in connected speech or writing, forming the grammatically-complex expression of a single thought'. A sentence must have parts, presumably what the *OED* means by complex. These parts must be identified and named if their behaviour is to be understood. The naming of the parts of speech, the parsing of sentences, is thus a practical task of learning. Syntax, the parts of speech, the disciplines and tricks that are the 'expression of a single thought', are crucial to a pupil's development. They are like driving a car, drawing up a budget or accessing a computer. The American writer Eudora Welty recalled in her autobiography how she was taught the 'beautiful accretion of the sentence'. It would, she said, 'finally stand there as real, intact and built to stay as the Mississippi State Capitol . . . under foot the echo of its marble floor and above the bell of its rotunda'. Nor is grammar a subject that can be learnt on the job. It has flexibility, problems, even dialects. It is the source of rich argument and controversy. But those who wish to learn it must be taught.

In spite of the blame that is heaped on newspapers for the state of the English language, they must of necessity remain committed to clear expression. Newspaper sentences, like their headlines, have to be instantly comprehensible. Instilled in every journalist – or at least in that hero of plain English, the sub-editor – is the principle of brevity, of short words and sentences, emphatic punctuation and simple grammar. Of how many government departments or corporate headquarters, how many schools or universities, could this be said? How many possess that Mrs Grundy of every newspaper office, a house style guide? Use Anglo-Saxon words not Latin ones – they are shorter. Avoid abstract nouns wherever possible – and avoid fuzzy thinking. Make verbs transitive not intransitive – they punch harder. Carry the imagery on verbs and nouns, not on adverbs and adjectives. Always read through what you have written and shorten it. Keep Fowler and Gowers, those masters of style, by your side. Disagree with them if you must, but know why you do so.

Many people have genuine difficulty expressing an idea or a message on paper. They do not find the English language an easy tool. Even those whose profession is to manipulate words can experience writer's block, made worse, I believe, by the video screen. I have watched people wrestle with a sentence as if it were a gorgon. They hack at one part of it and another comes behind them and grasps their throat. Sometimes I have helped with the first aid kit. Try to speak what you want to say before writing it down. Tell who did what to whom, where and when in the first sentence. Cross out every adverb and adjective. Use only full stops. Yet many troubled souls are still floundering. They know what they want to say. They have the words to hand. But they are driving without a road map. They race to every turning and then stop to search for signs, mystified at why it is taking them so long to get from A to B. They have not learnt grammar.

Grammar makes us masters of language, not its slaves. It builds up the intellectual muscles. It helps us engage in T.S. Eliot's 'intolerable wrestle with words and meanings'. Teachers and their pupils should be constantly on grammar alert. Kenneth Baker was right to blaze away with his twelve-bore. As that stern teacher Lewis Carroll asserted, 'The question is, Who is in charge?' To be always on the run before words is a humiliation and an unnecessary one. Words must be bent to our will. 'They've a temper, some of them,' cried Humpty-Dumpty, 'particularly the verbs, they're the proudest. Adjectives you can do anything with but not verbs. However, I can manage the whole lot of them!' He could and so should we.

INDEX